PSM 1

Workbook

Books published in PSM in 1984:

PSM 1a Sets I Symmetry Fractions I Measurement I
PSM 1b Fractions II Graphs and Functions I
Angles and Parallels Statistics I
PSM 1c Graphs and Functions II Fractions III
Primes and Indices Bearings
PSM 1d Measurement II Substitution Locus Fractions IV
PSM 1 Workbook
PSM 1 Teacher's Guide

PSM 1

Workbook

General Editor
Donald Stagg

Stanley Thornes (Publishers) Ltd

First published in 1984 by:

Stanley Thornes (Publishers) Ltd
Educa House
Old Station Drive
Leckhampton
CHELTENHAM GL53 0DN
England

British Library Cataloguing in Publication Data

PSM 1.
Workbook
1. Mathematics–1961-
I. Stagg, D.
510 QA39.2

ISBN 0-85950-170-1

Typeset by Tech-Set, Gateshead, Tyne & Wear, England.
Printed and bound in Great Britain at the Pitman Press, Bath, England.

CONTENTS

ACKNOWLEDGEMENTS

PSM was written by a group of experienced teachers.

Donald Stagg, Charterhouse (editor and chairman), Nigel Buckle, John Eadie, David Hanson, Mark Harvey, Nigel Kinloch, Martin Kneath, Shirley Lee and Jasper Selwyn

would like to thank the Trustees of the School Mathematics Project, and especially John Hersee, for their encouragement and support, and the following schools for their cooperation over testing material:

Downsend, Leatherhead
Castle Court School
Downsend Lodge
Marlborough College
Rowan Preparatory School
Aberlour House
Long Close School
The Pilgrims' School, Winchester
Charterhouse
Alleyn Court

1. SETS I

PRACTICE 1 (AB)

1

& = {Angus, Hamish, Fiona, John, Nicholas, Tom, Sarah, Richard, Philippa, Eve, Anne}

(These are all the children in a certain form.)

Write out the elements (some people call them members) of the following sets:

A = {girls}
B = {boys}
C = {children with an "n" in their name}
D = {children without an "n" in their name}
E = {children with 6 or more letters in their name}
F = {children whose names read the same backwards as forwards}

Now answer these questions:

a) Which children are in set C and in set E?

b) Which children aren't in set A or in set D?

c) A new child called Bob joins the form. Write down all the sets he should go in.

d) Copy the Venn diagram opposite and put each child in the correct place (including Bob).

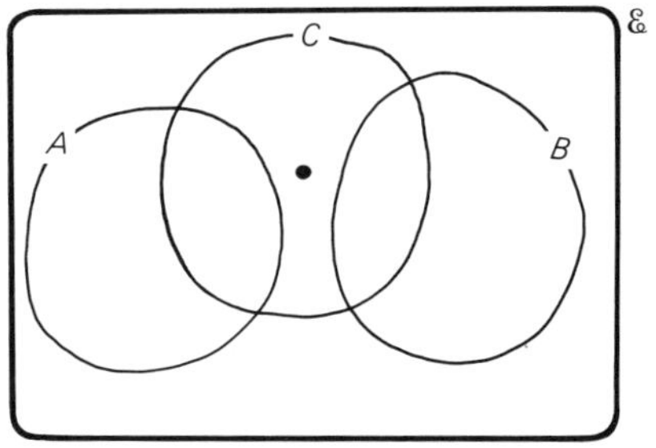

e) The area with a dot in it should not contain any names. Can you explain why?

2

Here are some sets of people:

$Q = \{$children$\}$
$R = \{$people who wear glasses$\}$
$S = \{$people with irritating voices$\}$
$T = \{$maths teachers$\}$
$U = \{$schoolboys$\}$
$V = \{$bad-tempered people$\}$
$W = \{$crazy people$\}$
$X = \{$people who wear short trousers$\}$
$Y = \{$teachers$\}$

Somebody who was in set T and in set V would be "a bad-tempered maths teacher". Somebody who was in set U but not in set R would be "a schoolboy who doesn't wear glasses". In the same way, describe people who are in set:

a) X and in set Y

b) Q but not in set U

c) Y but not in set T

d) R and in set Y and in set W

e) Y and in set S and in set V

f) W and in set Q but not in set U

g) T and in set W but not in set V.

3

$\mathscr{E} = \{\text{A, B, C, D, E, F, G, H}\}$

List the members of the following sets:

a) {letters with no round parts}

b) {letters with no straight parts}

c) {letters which are in the word MATHEMATICS}

4

$\mathscr{E} = \{1, 2, 3, 4, 5, 6, 7, 8, 9, 10\}$
$A = \{$even numbers$\}$
$B = \{$odd numbers$\}$

$C = \{$numbers that divide by 3 exactly, including 3 itself$\}$

$D = \{$numbers that can be written without taking your pen off the paper, and without going over any line twice$\}$

(If we were thinking of letters, P would be in set D but T would not.)

a) List the elements of the four sets.

b) Which numbers are in B and in C?

c) Which numbers are in A but not in C?

d) Which elements of B divide exactly into 105?

5

By the end of the day Professor Mildew's pockets are usually full to overflowing, so the first thing Mrs Mildew does when she gets up in the morning is to empty them. On a typical day she found this universal set:

ℰ = {
£1 note
jam doughnut
gob-stopper
protractor
50 p piece
hard-boiled egg
LP (long playing record)
Polo mint
cube
}

She put them on the dressing table and arranged them into a Venn diagram:

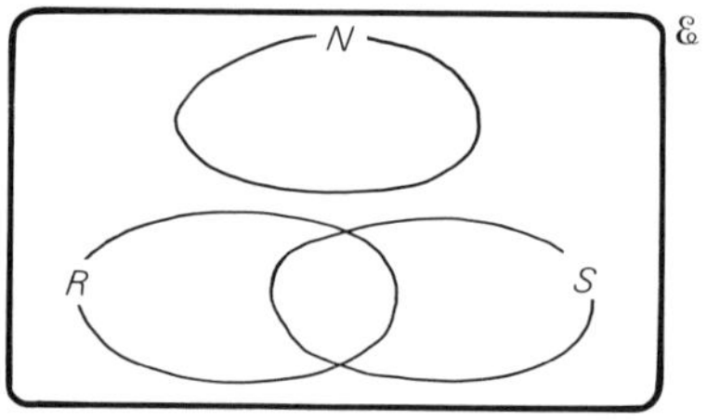

$N = \{$things having no edges$\}$
$R = \{$things with a round edge$\}$
$S = \{$things with a straight edge$\}$

(Of course she noticed that one of the things had a round edge *and* a straight edge.)

a) Make a *large* copy of the Venn diagram and put each thing in its correct place.

The first thing the Professor did when he got up was to arrange the things into a completely different Venn diagram:

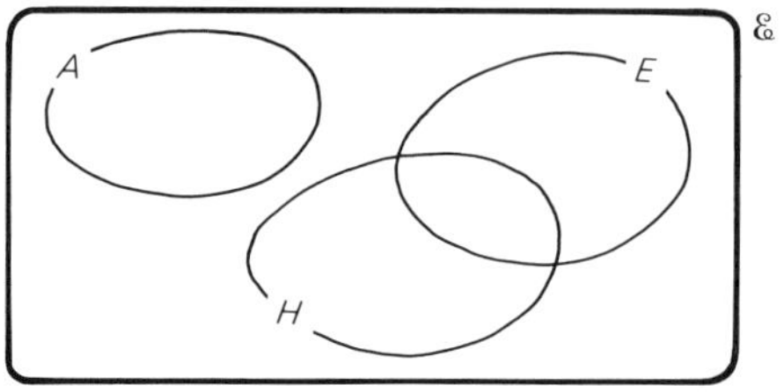

$E = \{$things you can eat$\}$
$H = \{$things with a hole in the middle$\}$
$A = \{$things with a right angle in them somewhere$\}$

(A few things don't belong to any of the three sets, but they still have their place in the Venn diagram.)

b) Make a *large* copy of this Venn diagram and put each thing in its correct place.

PRACTICE 2 (CDE)

1

& $= \{$all animals$\}$
$A = \{$animals that live in trees$\}$
$B = \{$animals weighing less than 1 kilogram$\}$

$C = \{\text{animals that can fly}\}$
$D = \{\text{elephants}\}$
$E = \{\text{children in your school}\}$
$F = \{\text{bees}\}$
$G = \{\text{animals with grey skin and long trunks}\}$
$H = \{\text{teachers}\}$
$I = \{\text{people who talk too much}\}$
$J = \{\text{animals that lay eggs}\}$

a) Write down which of these are empty sets:

$G \cap H$ $\quad A \cap B$ $\quad C \cap D$ $\quad E \cap J$ $\quad D \cap G$

$F \cap C$ $\quad B \cap C'$ $\quad D \cap G'$ $\quad H \cap I$ $\quad J \cap A$

$C \cap B'$ $\quad E' \cap H'$

b) Write down which of these statements are true:

$F \subset C$ $\quad D \subset B$ $\quad D \subset J'$ $\quad J \subset \{\text{chickens}\}$

mouse $\in B'$

c) Name an animal that would be in each of these sets:

$B \cap C$ $\quad J \cap B'$ $\quad E \cap I$ (no marks for this one!)

2

$\mathscr{E} = \{l, u, n, a, t, i, c, s\}$
$P = \{s, a, i, n, t\}$
$Q = \{s, i, n\}$
$R = \{a, u, n, t\}$

List the members of the following sets:

a) P' **b)** $Q \cap R$ **c)** Q' **d)** $Q' \cap R$

e) $P \cap R$ **f)** $(P \cap R)'$

3

Copy the Venn diagram and put each number in its correct place:

$\mathscr{E} = \{3, 4, 5, 6, 7, 8, 9\}$
$A = \{5, 6, 7\}$
$B = \{6, 7\}$
$C = \{8, 9\}$

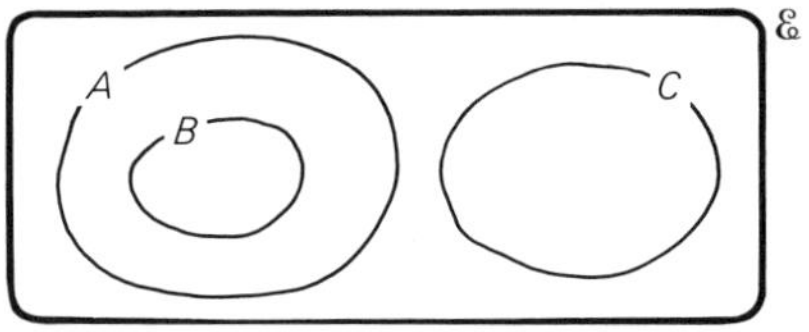

4

$\mathscr{E} = \{d, i, s, t, a, n, c, e\}$
$X = \{c, a, n, e\}$
$Y = \{c, a, t\}$
$Z = \{i, s\}$

a) Draw a Venn diagram and put each letter in its correct place.

b) List the members of Y'.

c) Is it true or false to say that $Z \subset Y'$?

d) List the members of $Y' \cap X$.

5

$\mathscr{E} = \{m, a, s, t, e, r\}$
$F = \{s, t, a, r\}$
$G = \{m, e\}$
$H = \{r, a, t\}$

Copy down the following, putting one of the set symbols ($\in$, $\cap$, $\subset$, $\emptyset$) in place of the dots to make a true statement:

a) $F \cap G = \ldots$ b) $H \ldots F$ c) $\text{m} \ldots G$

d) $G \ldots H = \emptyset$ e) $\text{e} \ldots F'$ f) $\{\text{m}\} \ldots G$

6

A number of people at Subset House School were asked to draw a Venn diagram showing these sets:

$\mathscr{E}$ = {people}
S = {show-offs}
B = {boys at Subset House}

Emma snorted and drew this Venn diagram:

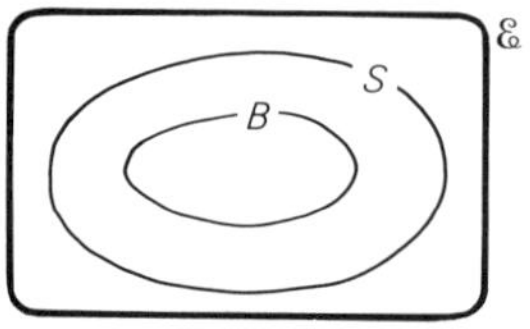

Angus said it was obvious that this was the answer:

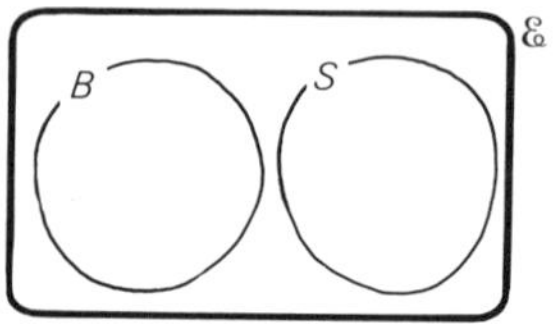

Mr Abel, their teacher, drew this:

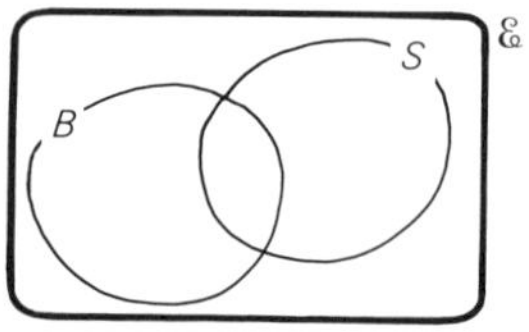

Explain in a sentence what each of them is saying by the Venn diagram he or she has drawn.

SUMMARY

1

$\mathscr{E} = \{*, '', ?, /, @, £, \&, \%, +\}$
$P = \{?, £, \%, +\}$
$Q = \{*, ?, @, \&, +\}$

a) How many elements has $P \cap Q$?

b) List the elements of $P \cap Q'$.

c) Set R has two elements and is such that $R \subset P$ and $R \cap Q = \emptyset$. List the elements of R.

2

There are 12 children in Form V. Three of them are both stupid and ugly, and *altogether* there are eight stupid children. Two children are neither stupid nor ugly.

Copy the Venn diagram opposite and put the correct numbers in each area. Work out how many children are ugly but not stupid.

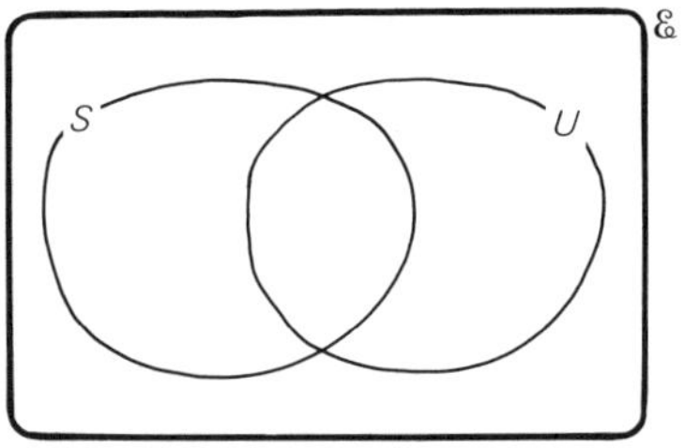

3

For each part of this question make a new copy of the Venn diagram.

Shade the area corresponding to:

a) B' b) $A \cap B'$

c) $(A \cap B)'$

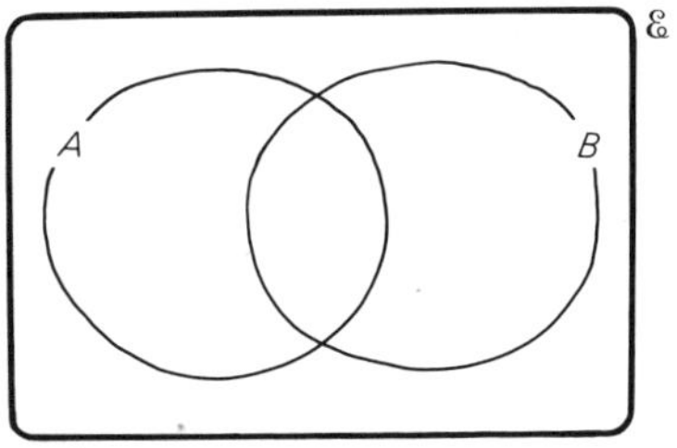

4

A factor of a number is another number which divides into it.

factors of 28 = {1 and 28, 2 and 14, 4 and 7}

Notice that 1 and 28 do themselves count as factors. Write the factors in pairs like this so as not to miss any.

a) List the elements of {factors of 45}.

b) List the elements of {factors of 60}.

c) Use your answers to (a) and (b) to find the factors which are common to both 45 and 60.

ALLSORTS

1

A foul murder has been commited at Hyperbola Hall, the stately home of the Connick-Section family. According to Inspector Brass, who is in charge of the case, the only people who could have committed the crime are:

& = {Reverend Chicken, Miss Gargle, Lady Twittering, Colonel Blimp, Dr Foulenough, Aunt Beatrice, Slobber the butler, Dotty the cook}

"Hmmm," muttered the Inspector. "Whoever did it must have had an axe or a meat-cleaver, and the strength to use it. They can't have had an alibi, of course." (An alibi is a proof that you were somewhere else when the crime was committed.)

The set of people who had an axe with them is:

X = {Reverend Chicken, Dr Foulenough, Lady Twittering}

The set of people who had a meat-cleaver is:

M = {Dr Foulenough, Colonel Blimp, Slobber}

The set of people with the strength to deliver the blow is:

S = {Dotty, Reverend Chicken, Slobber, Aunt Beatrice}

The set of people with an alibi is:

A = {Colonel Blimp, Reverend Chicken, Lady Twittering}

Who is the only person who could have committed the murder?

2

$\mathscr{E} = \{9, 10, 11, 12, 13, 14, 15, 16, 17, 18\}$

A = {numbers that divide exactly by 2}

B = {numbers that divide exactly by 3}

C = {numbers that divide exactly by 4}

D = {numbers that divide exactly by 6}

a) List sets A, B, C and D.

b) A certain number belongs to precisely two of these sets – no more and no less. What is it?

c) Another number belongs to precisely three of these sets. What is it?

3

In the Sets Game you are given a letter of the alphabet, and you have to write down a set of words which all begin with this letter. The elements of the set must be a country, a girl's name, a tree, a town or city in Britain and an animal. As an example:

P = { Poland, Penny, pine, Pontefract, pig }

Try to write out examples of these sets:

a) L **b)** A **c)** H

2. SYMMETRY

If a photocopier is available, copies may be taken of the diagrams on pp. 11, 12, 13, 15, 16.

*Note: copyright is waived on these diagrams only.

PRACTICE 1 (A)

1

Don't copy the diagrams below, just write down how many lines of symmetry each one has.

a)

b)

c)

d)

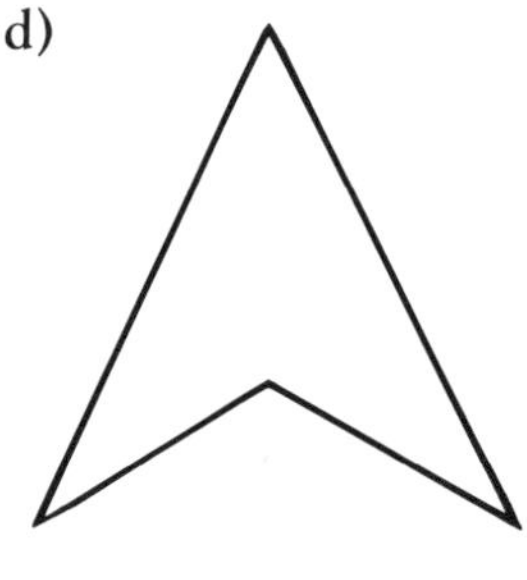

e)

f)

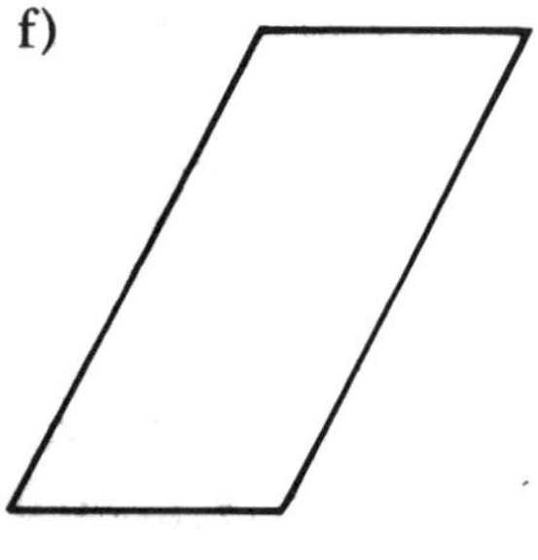

g)

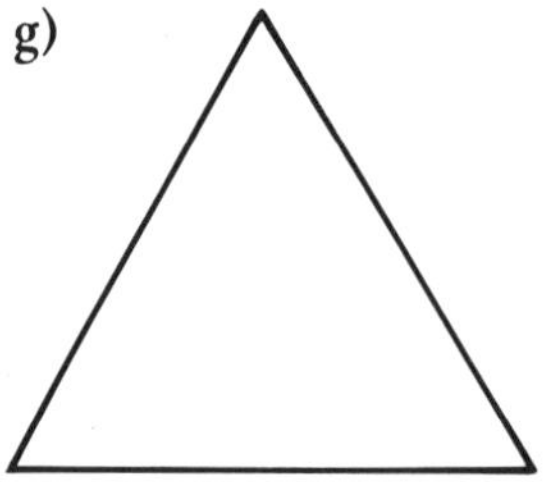

2

Copy the diagrams on the next page as neatly and carefully as you can (use a photocopy or tracing paper) and mark all the lines of symmetry with *dotted* lines.

a)

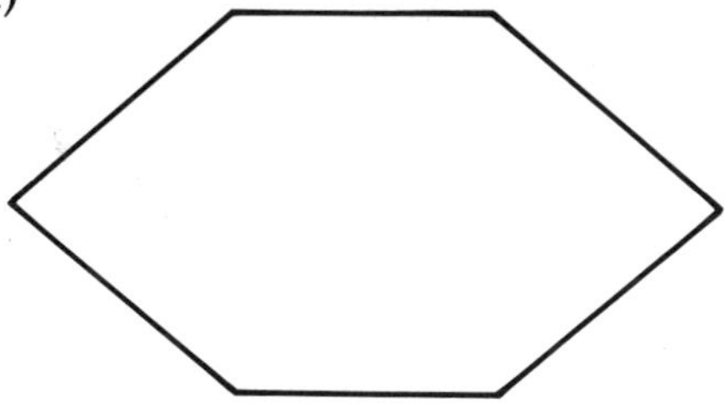

b)

c)

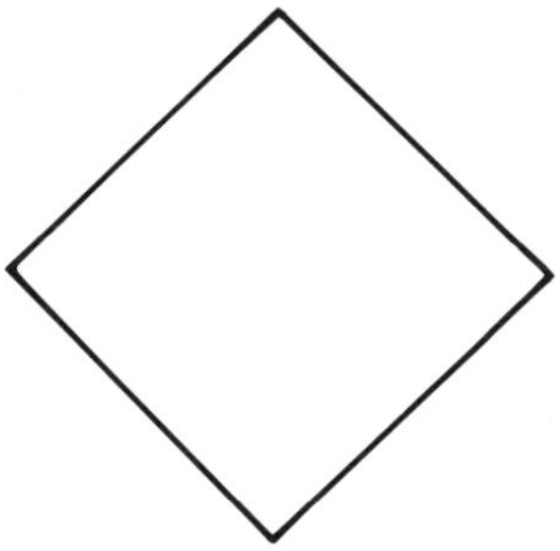

d)

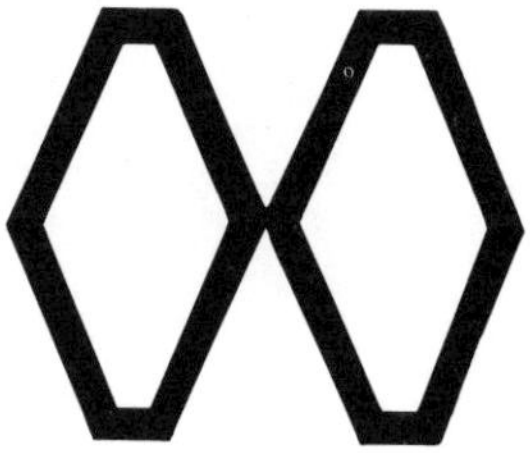

e)

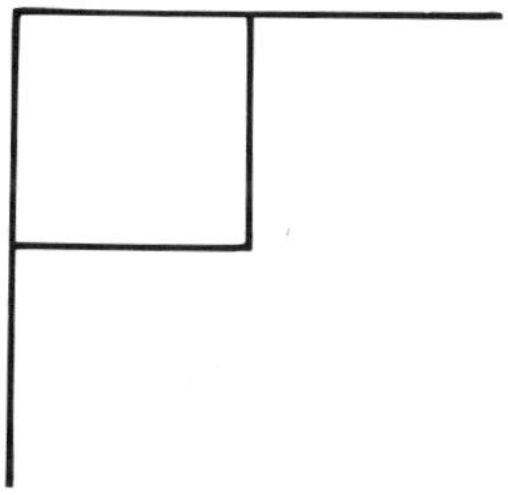

f)

3

Look at the *alphabet below*, and write down all the letters which have no lines of symmetry.

A B C D E F G H I J K L M N O P Q R S T U V W X Y Z

4

Copy the diagrams carefully (use a photocopy or tracing paper) and complete them so that the dotted line is a line of symmetry.

a)

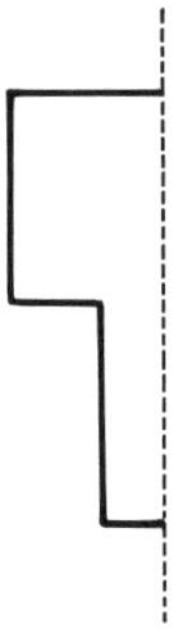

b)

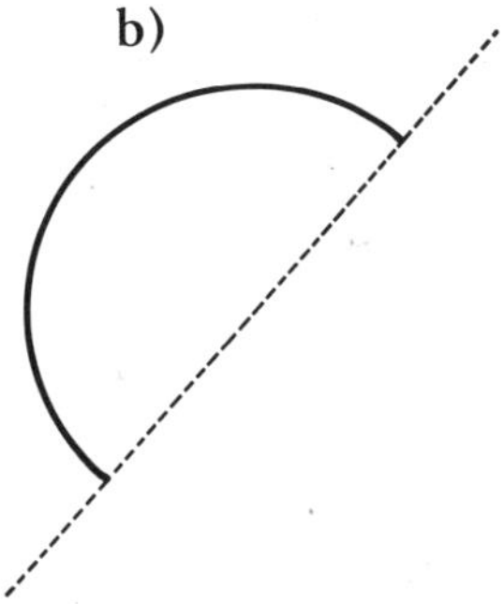

c)

d)

e)

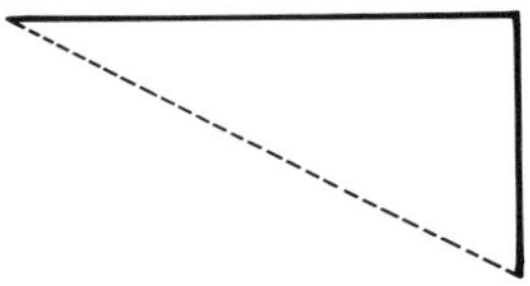

5

Copy the diagrams below carefully (use a photocopy or trace them if possible) and add the *least* number of lines needed to give each diagram a line of symmetry. Then mark the lines of symmetry with dotted lines.

For example, if the diagram is  the best answer is 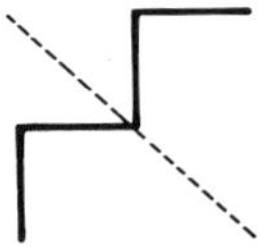

a)

b)

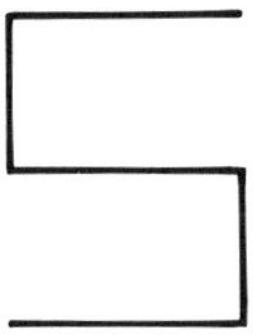

c)

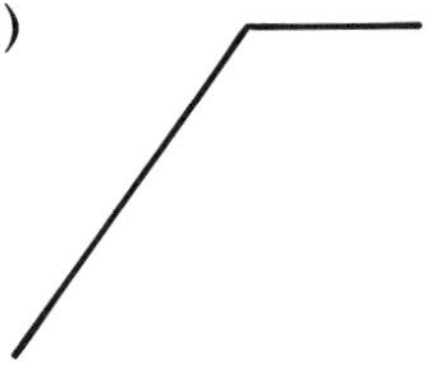

d)

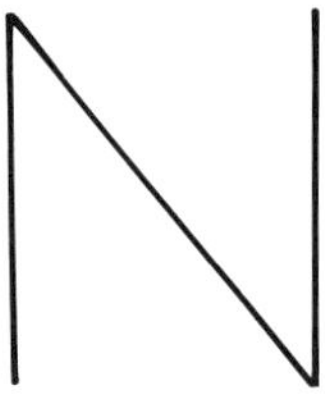

e)

f)

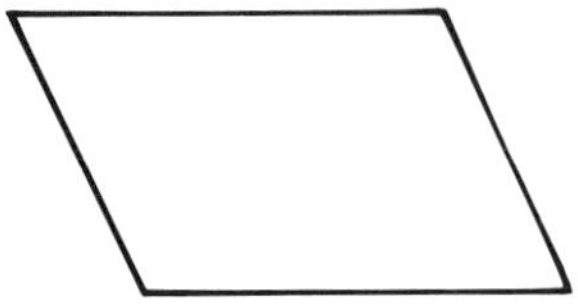

g)

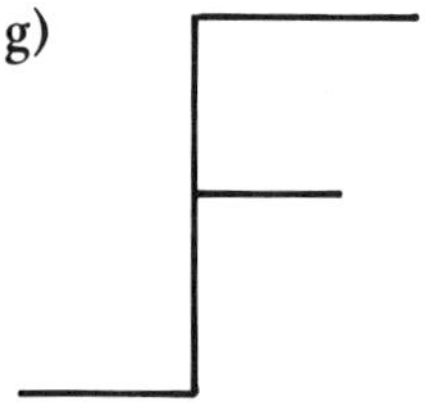

PRACTICE 2 (BC)

1

Don't copy the diagrams below, just write down what order of rotational symmetry each one has. Remember, if it has no rotational symmetry, it is of order 1.

a)

b)

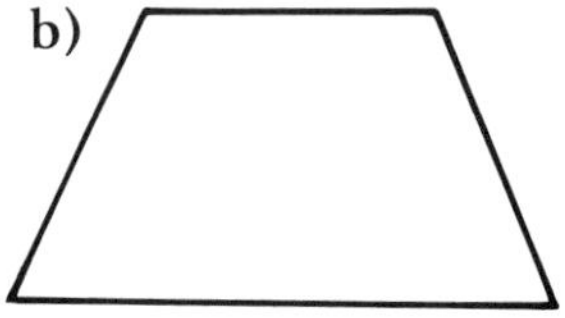

c)

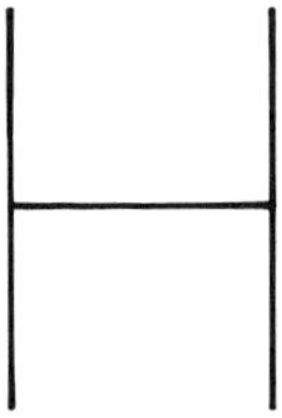

d) 

e) 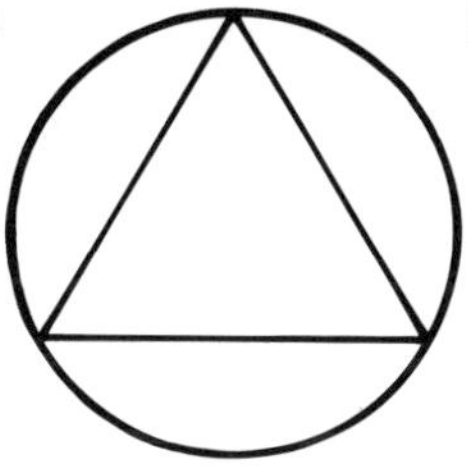

f) 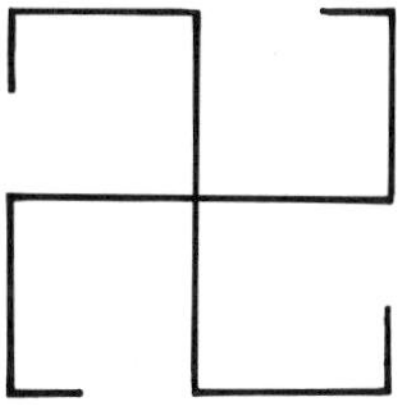

g) 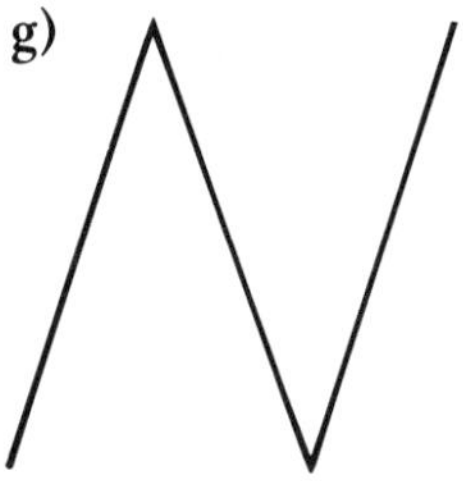

h) 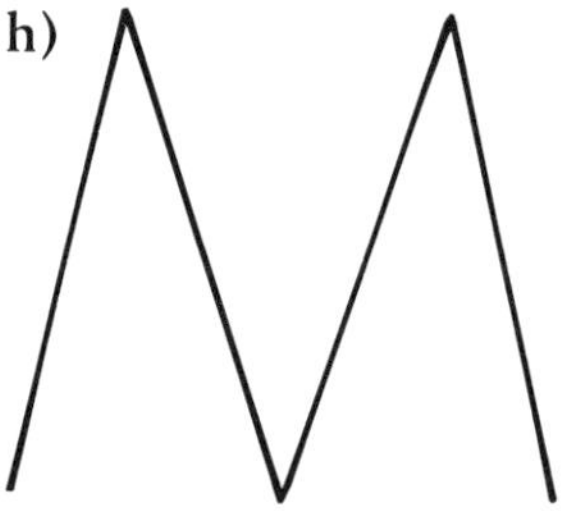

2

Using the squares in your book to help you, copy the diagram below exactly. Then complete it so that it has rotational symmetry of the order given in brackets, with the dot as the centre of symmetry.

Two examples are given to help you understand what the question means:

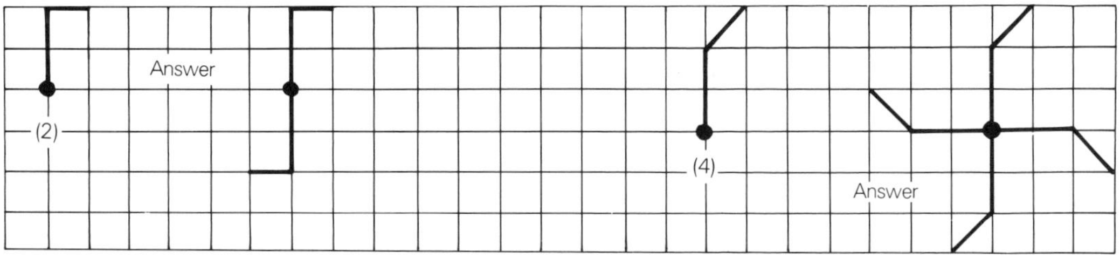

Now do these yourself:

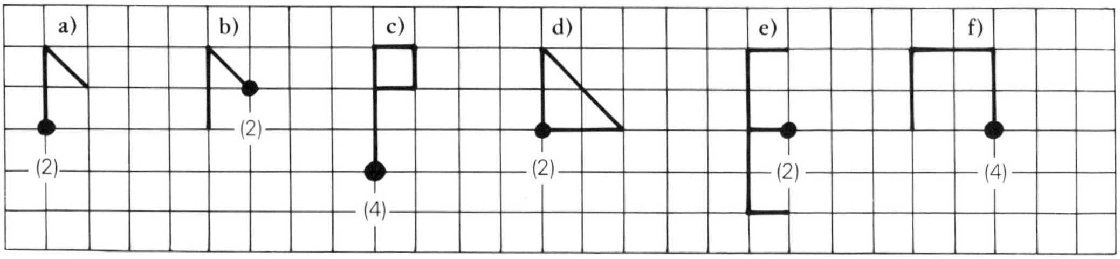

3

Don't copy the diagrams on the next page, but write down how many lines of symmetry each one has, and also what order of rotational symmetry each one has.

Your answer might look like this:

No lines of symmetry.

Rotational symmetry of order 4.

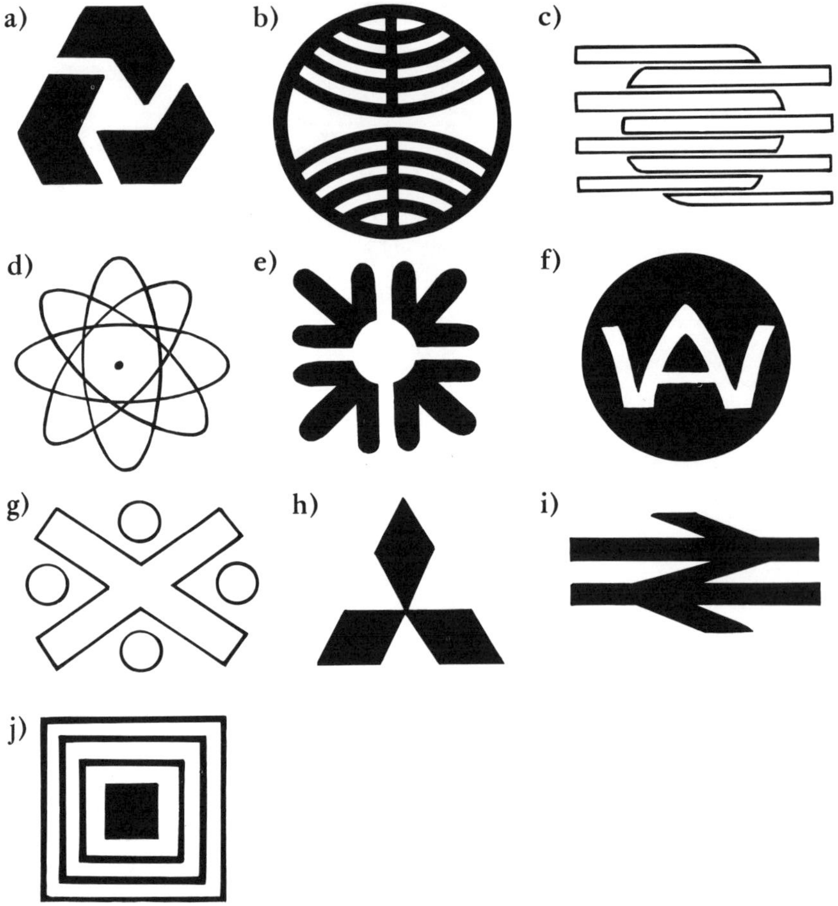

(These are all registered trade marks.)

4

Neatly and carefully draw diagrams which have the following symmetry. One of them is impossible to draw – say which one it is.

a) 1 line of symmetry; rotational symmetry of order 1.

b) No lines of symmetry; rotational symmetry of order 2.

c) 2 lines of symmetry; rotational symmetry of order 1.

d) No lines of symmetry; rotational symmetry of order 3.

e) 4 lines of symmetry; rotational symmetry of order 4.

5

You probably know how numbers are formed on a digital watch or a calculator. They are all formed by using some of the lines of a double square.

From this outline 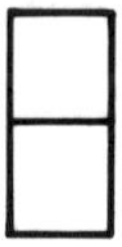 we can make 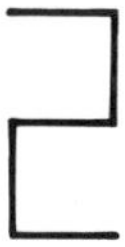 or  or any other number.

2 4

Working down the page in a column, make a list of all the numbers from 0 to 9 as seen on a digital watch. Make them the same size as the ones above. Beside each number, write how many lines of symmetry it has and what order of rotational symmetry it has.

The sum on the right is correct, but it is written as it would be seen in a mirror. Rewrite it as it really is.

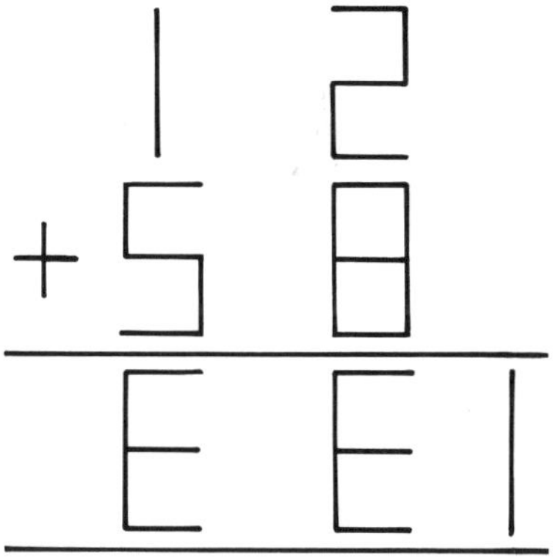

SUMMARY

1

Copy carefully (or trace) the diagrams below, and complete them so that they have the symmetry stated.

a)  Rotational symmetry of order 4 about the dot.

b) 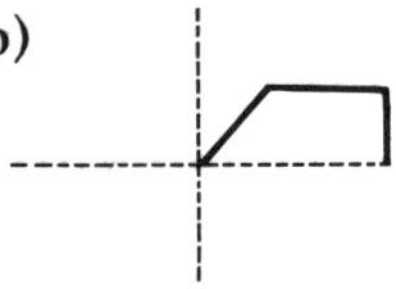 Both dotted lines are to be lines of symmetry.

c) 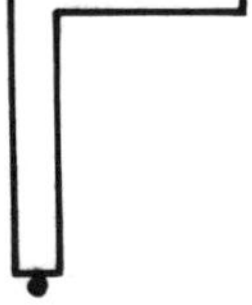 Rotational symmetry of order 3 about the dot.

d) 

Complete with the least number of lines so that the diagram has rotational symmetry of order 2 about the dot *and* 2 lines of symmetry.

2

Describe the symmetry – line and rotational – of each of these diagrams:

a)

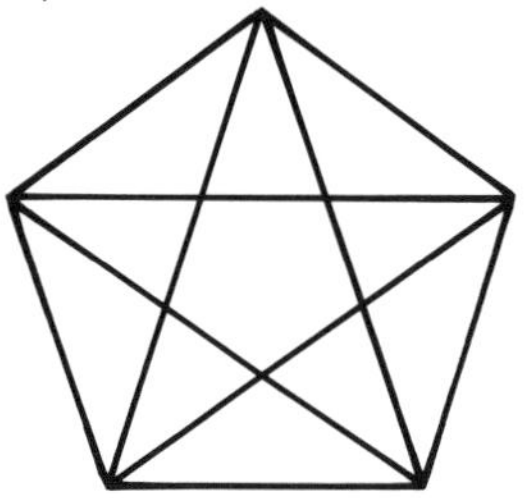

b)

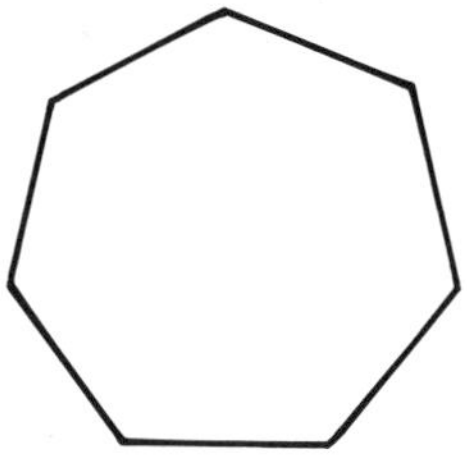

c)

d)

e)

SWIMS

f)

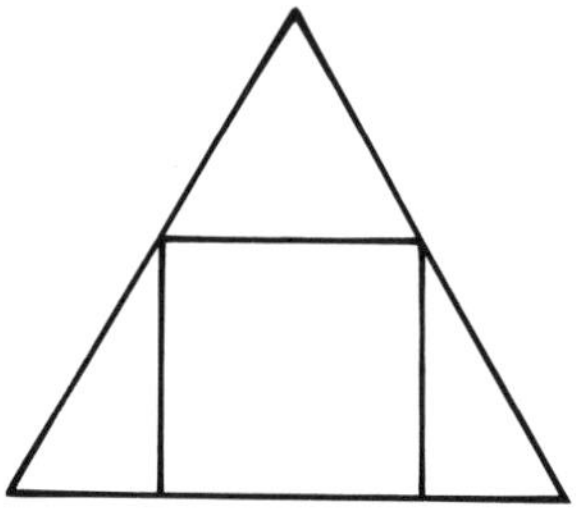

((c) and (d) are registered trade marks.)

3

Look at this alphabet:

A B C D E F G H I J K L M N O P Q R S T U V W X Y Z

Some of the letters have a *vertical* line of symmetry like A.

Some of the letters have a *horizontal* line of symmetry like K.

Make a list of all the letters that have vertical lines of symmetry, and a separate list of all the letters that have horizontal lines of symmetry. Notice that a few letters have a horizontal and a vertical line of symmetry, so they will appear in both lists.

We can make whole words that have lines of symmetry:

Vertical

Horizontal

Using your lists to help you, find the longest word you can which has a vertical line of symmetry, then the longest you can which has a horizontal line of symmetry.

4

You have 12 matchsticks to use in each part of this question, and you must use them all. If you had to make a shape with rotational symmetry of order 2 and no lines of symmetry you could make one like this:

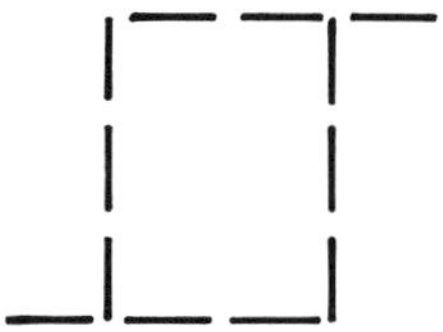

Make similar shapes which have:

a) 4 lines of symmetry and rotational symmetry of order 4.

b) 1 line of symmetry and rotational symmetry of order 1.

c) No lines of symmetry and rotational symmetry of order 3.

d) 6 lines of symmetry and rotational symmetry of order 6.

ALLSORTS

1

There had been another ghastly murder at Hyperbola Hall (there's one most weekends). The only clue Inspector Brass has been able to find is a piece of blotting paper with two things written on it. The first is in capitals so it is fairly easy to read even without a mirror:

The second is in ordinary writing, which is a bit harder:

Can you read the two sentences?

2

The President of the Republic of Mania has decided to have a new flag for the country and he wants a symbol to go on it. He has decided that the symbol must have a circle and at least one isosceles triangle in it. It must have at least one letter M (for Mania), but it must not have any right angles. Finally, the whole thing must have rotational symmetry or order 4.

The palace designer produced this symbol, for which he was promptly executed because it is wrong in two ways:

(i) It doesn't have rotational symmetry of order 4.

(ii) It does have a right angle in it.

Can you find a design that fits all the President's wishes?

3

How many different patterns can you make using 4 squares joined together, either edge to edge or corner to corner? Here are some examples:

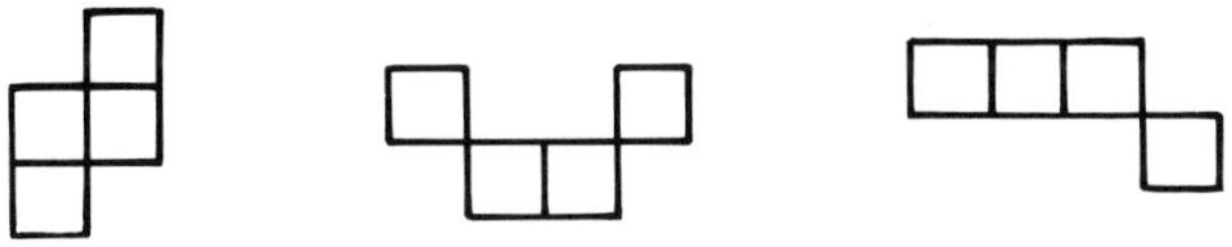

Some patterns that look different are really the same, but turned round or turned over:

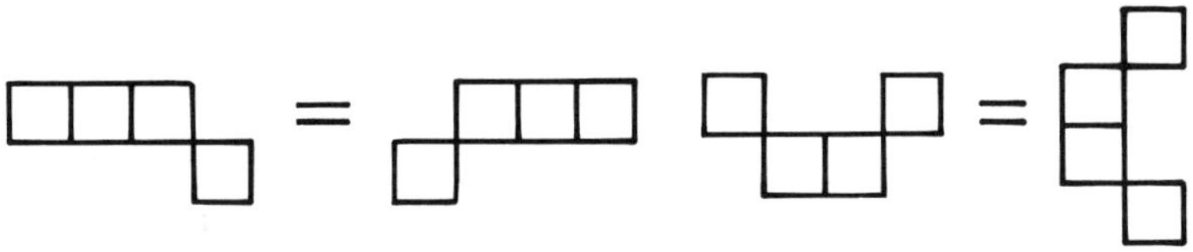

When you have found as many patterns as you can, go back and write an L beside each one that has a line of symmetry, and an R beside each one that has rotational symmetry. (Some patterns will get an L and an R, of course.)

Note: There are more than 20 shapes. They will look nicer coloured in or shaded.

3. FRACTIONS I

PRACTICE 1 (ABC)

1

a) When there is a school outing Mrs Haddock, the cook, gives each child a quarter of a pork pie. One day, when the hamper came back afterwards, she found that 7 children had not eaten their pieces. If she put the 7 pieces together, how many whole pies would she have? Give your answer as a mixed number.

b) On another outing she only had enough pies to give each child a fifth of a pork pie. The same 7 children didn't eat their pieces. How many whole pork pies would she be able to make with the leftovers this time?

2

Turn these improper fractions into mixed numbers:

a) $\frac{7}{6}$ b) $\frac{11}{3}$ c) $\frac{8}{5}$ d) $\frac{14}{9}$ e) $\frac{9}{4}$

f) $\frac{16}{5}$ g) $\frac{7}{2}$

3

a) Mrs Haddock has $3\frac{3}{4}$ pork pies in her pantry. How many quarters will she be able to cut from them?

b) If she had $2\frac{1}{3}$ pies, how many thirds of a pie would she be able to cut?

4

Copy the following questions, putting the correct number in place of the question mark:

a) $1\frac{3}{4} = \frac{?}{4}$ b) $2\frac{2}{5} = \frac{?}{5}$ c) $1\frac{1}{8} = \frac{?}{8}$ d) $3\frac{1}{3} = \frac{?}{3}$

e) $3\frac{1}{5} = \frac{?}{5}$ f) $5\frac{5}{6} = \frac{?}{6}$ g) $2\frac{1}{2} = \frac{?}{2}$ h) $4\frac{1}{4} = \frac{?}{4}$

5

Copy the following questions, putting the correct number in place of the question mark:

a) $\frac{2}{3} = \frac{?}{9}$ b) $\frac{4}{5} = \frac{?}{20}$ c) $\frac{5}{8} = \frac{?}{16}$ d) $\frac{1}{3} = \frac{?}{12}$

e) $\frac{2}{9} = \frac{?}{18}$ f) $\frac{6}{7} = \frac{?}{21}$ g) $\frac{3}{4} = \frac{?}{24}$ h) $\frac{1}{4} = \frac{?}{20}$

i) $\frac{2}{3} = \frac{?}{6} = \frac{?}{12} = \frac{?}{18} = \frac{?}{24} = \frac{?}{60} = \frac{?}{300}$

6

Do these adding and subtracting sums:

a) $\frac{7}{12} + \frac{1}{3}$ b) $\frac{3}{4} - \frac{1}{16}$ c) $\frac{5}{9} - \frac{1}{3}$ d) $\frac{3}{5} + \frac{1}{10}$

e) $\frac{2}{3}-\frac{2}{15}$ f) $\frac{2}{5}+\frac{3}{20}$ g) $\frac{3}{4}+\frac{1}{16}$ h) $\frac{7}{10}-\frac{2}{5}$

7

Mrs Haddock had been having trouble with her pork pies again. She had been giving the children a quarter of a pie each in their packed lunches, when to her horror she found she needed 5 more slices and only had $\frac{3}{4}$ of a pie left. Even she knew enough maths to realise that you can only get three quarters from $\frac{3}{4}$ (if you see what I mean).

Mr Abel, the maths teacher, happened to be passing and he tried to explain how to attack the problem mathematically. But when he started talking about mixed numbers, Mrs Haddock cried, "I don't know nothing about mixed numbers. Mixed spices is good enough for me." And she shooed him out of the kitchen.

Then she set about the problem herself. First she cut off a slice which, though she didn't know it, was exactly $\frac{3}{20}$ of the pie. When she had done that there was $\frac{3}{4}-\frac{3}{20}$ of the pie left.

a) Do the subtraction.

b) If she cuts slices the same size as the first, work out what fraction of the pie would be left after she had cut:
2 slices,
3 slices,
4 slices,
from the pie.

c) Will Mrs Haddock be able to get 5 equal slices in the end?

PRACTICE 2 (DEFGH)

1

Write down what fraction of each of the following shapes has been shaded. Then write your answer in its simplest form (if it can be made simpler).

a) 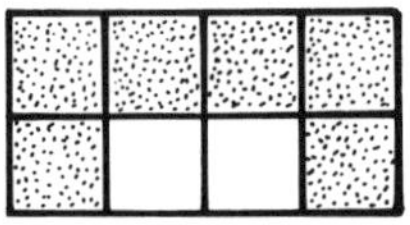

b) 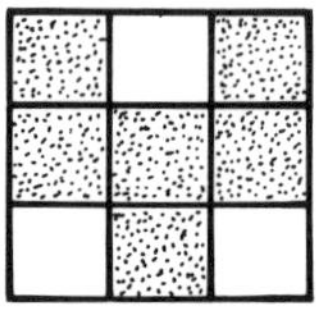

c) 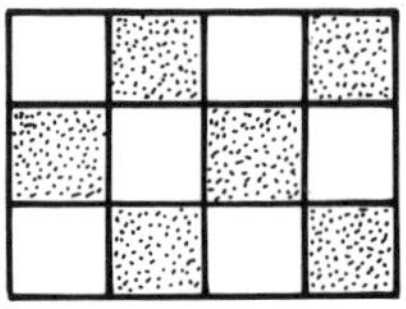

d)

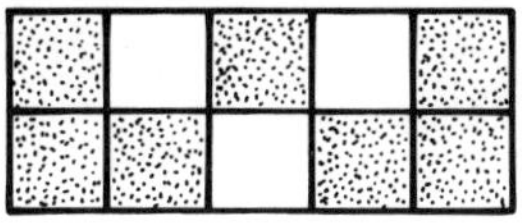

e)

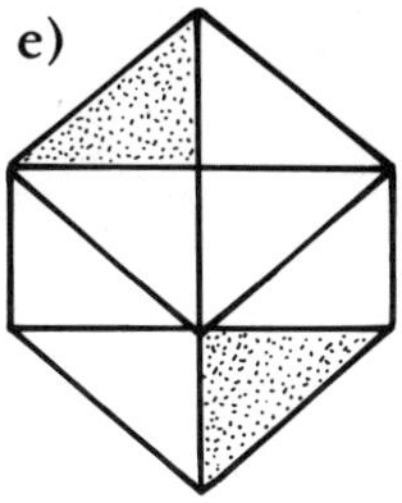

f)

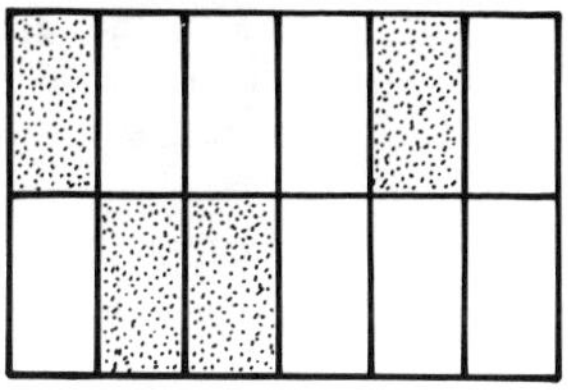

g)

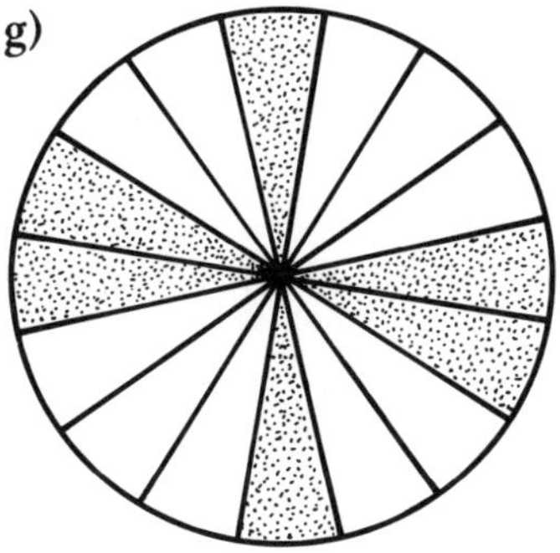

h)

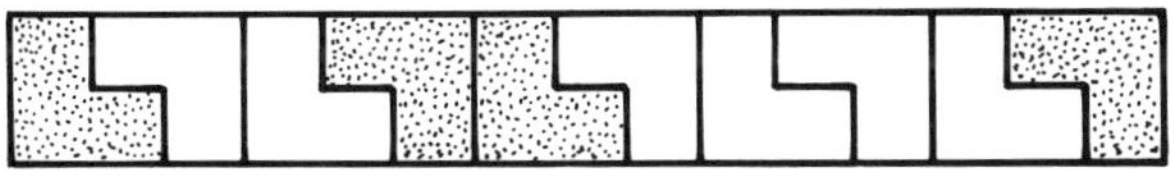

i)

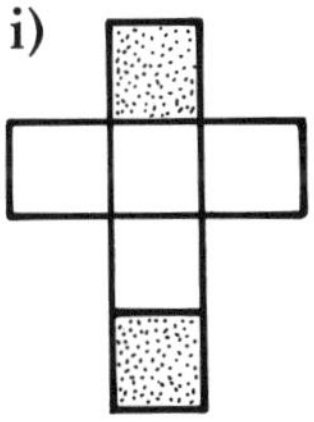

j)

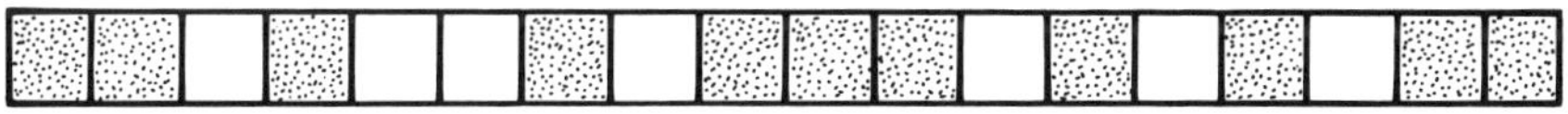

2

Add these fractions, remembering to give your answer in its simplest form:

a) $\frac{2}{3}+\frac{1}{4}$ b) $\frac{1}{3}+\frac{1}{6}$ c) $\frac{3}{5}+\frac{1}{15}$ d) $\frac{1}{2}+\frac{2}{7}$

e) $\frac{1}{4}+\frac{2}{5}$ f) $\frac{2}{5}+\frac{1}{10}$ g) $\frac{1}{6}+\frac{1}{9}$ h) $\frac{1}{12}+\frac{2}{3}$

3

Add these mixed numbers:

a) $2\frac{2}{3}+3\frac{5}{6}$ b) $4\frac{3}{5}+1\frac{9}{10}$ c) $2\frac{1}{3}+6\frac{5}{9}$ d) $1\frac{7}{12}+1\frac{3}{4}$

e) $3\frac{3}{4}+2\frac{5}{8}$ f) $2\frac{3}{5}+4\frac{1}{2}$

4

Do these subtraction sums:

a) $5\frac{3}{4} - 2\frac{7}{12}$ b) $4\frac{1}{4} - 1\frac{7}{8}$ c) $8\frac{1}{2} - 5\frac{7}{10}$ d) $8\frac{1}{3} - 2\frac{7}{9}$

e) $3\frac{4}{15} - 1\frac{1}{3}$ f) $4\frac{5}{7} - 2\frac{1}{2}$

5

Find:

a) $\frac{2}{3}$ of £75 b) $\frac{5}{6}$ of 510 metres

c) $\frac{3}{4}$ of 76 p d) $\frac{3}{8}$ of £1000

6

Replace the question marks with the correct sign, $<$ or $>$, in the following:

a) $\frac{2}{3} \; ? \; \frac{3}{4}$ b) $\frac{5}{8} \; ? \; \frac{3}{4}$ c) $\frac{1}{6} \; ? \; \frac{2}{15}$ d) $\frac{6}{7} \; ? \; \frac{11}{14}$

e) $\frac{7}{12} \; ? \; \frac{25}{48}$ f) $\frac{17}{20} \; ? \; \frac{43}{50}$

7

A poor old farmer had three sons. When he died, his will said he wanted his belongings divided up in this way:

$\frac{1}{2}$ to the eldest son; $\frac{1}{3}$ to the middle son; $\frac{1}{9}$ to the youngest son.

After the debts had been paid, all that was left over was a herd of 17 cows. Now 2 doesn't go into 17 exactly, nor does 3, nor does 9. The three sons couldn't agree how to divide things up.

After a lot of arguing they took the matter to the wisest man in the village. He said, "I'll think it over and find a solution by tomorrow."

Next day the wise man called on the brothers, leading a cow of his own behind him. "Put this one with the other cows in the field and divide the herd of 18 according to the will," he said. The brothers replied, "But you can't afford to give us a cow – you're not a rich man either." The wise man just smiled and said, "Don't worry – I won't lose out in the end."

a) So the eldest brother took $\frac{1}{2}$ of the herd. How many cows was this?

b) The middle brother took $\frac{1}{3}$ of the herd. How many did he get?

c) Finally the youngest brother took his share: $\frac{1}{9}$ of the 18 cows. How many did he get?

d) Why didn't the wise man lose out in the end?

SUMMARY

1

Dr Ivel, the Headmaster of Subset House School, hates prime numbers. He only likes numbers which have lots of factors (numbers which divide into them).

For this reason, lessons and preps at Subset House all last for precisely 48 minutes (lots of numbers divide into 48!). The laziest boy in the school spent his prep in this way:

$\frac{1}{4}$ of the time whispering to his neighbour,

$\frac{1}{6}$ of the time staring out of the window,

$\frac{3}{8}$ of the time drawing aeroplanes in the back of his book,

$\frac{1}{12}$ of the time changing the cartridge in his pen.

The rest of the time he was working. How many minutes did he spend whispering, staring, drawing and changing his cartridge? How many minutes did he spend working?

2

Add: $3\frac{1}{3} + 2\frac{5}{6} + 1\frac{1}{4}$

3

Subtract: $8 - 4\frac{2}{9}$ (**Hint**: 8 can be written as $7 + \frac{9}{9}$.)

4

a) Copy the following questions and put the correct number in place of the question mark:

$$\frac{3}{8} = \frac{?}{24}$$

$$\frac{1}{3} = \frac{?}{24}$$

Which is larger, $\frac{3}{8}$ or $\frac{1}{3}$?

b) Thinking how you did question (a), find out which is larger, $\frac{3}{5}$ or $\frac{2}{3}$.

5

Add: $\frac{1}{2}+\frac{1}{3}+\frac{1}{4}+\frac{1}{5}+\frac{1}{6}$. (**Hint**: the smallest number that 2, 3, 4, 5 and 6 all divide into is 60.)

6

To start with there were 10 teacakes on the table. Fatima took $\frac{1}{2}$ a teacake, Tom took a whole one, and liked it so much he had another $\frac{1}{4}$; then the twins came in and had $\frac{3}{4}$ of a teacake each; Hamish had one too, and sneaked another $\frac{1}{2}$ teacake into his pocket for later. How many teacakes were left on the table?

ALLSORTS

1

Tom, Hamish and Emma had a packet of sweets to share between themselves. Unfortunately there were 32 sweets in the packet, and they all realised that 3 doesn't go into 32.

"I know," said Tom, "I'll take half of them, Emma can take half of what's left, Hamish can take half of what's left then, I'll take half again, and so on. If we're each taking half all the time, it's got to be fair."

Emma wasn't sure, and she saw another snag. "What about when we get down to the last sweet. Are we going to start cutting it into halves and quarters?"

"No," said Tom, "when we get down to the last one, the person whose turn it is can have it all."

Emma still wasn't convinced, and started to work out what each of them would get under Tom's "fair" system. What answers did she find?

2

The diagram opposite shows a chess-board.

● stands for a black piece.

○ stands for a white piece.

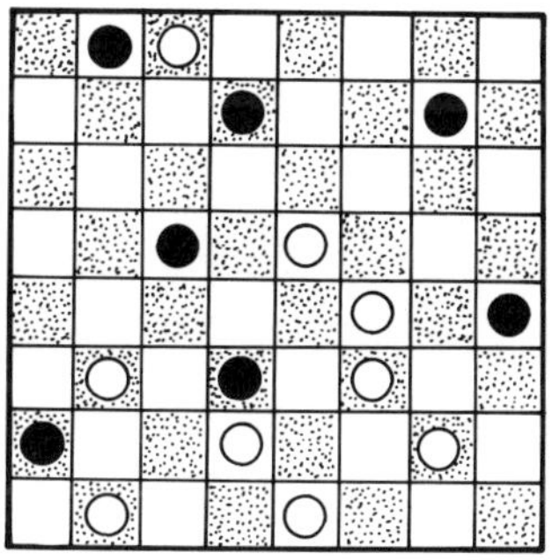

Simplifying your answers if possible, find:

a) What fraction of all the squares have a piece on them?

b) What fraction of the white squares have a white piece on them?

c) What fraction of the white squares don't have any piece on them?

3

Egbert is greedy little boy. He has just bought a cake and wants to cut it into 12 pieces so that he can eat a piece every hour from when he gets up until he goes to bed.

Egbert is also a lazy little boy. He realises there are different ways in which he could cut the cake into 12 pieces, and wonders which one needs the least number of cuts.

Here is his cake:

He could cut it like this, which would take 11 cuts:

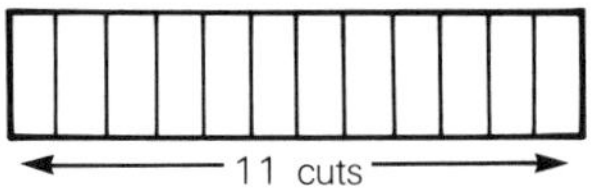

Or like this, which would take 6 cuts altogether:

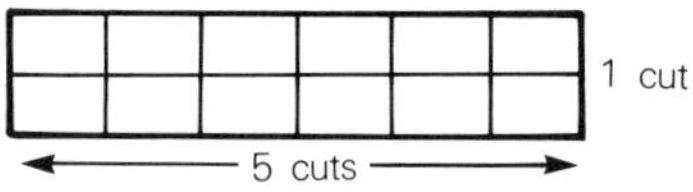

Can you think of a quicker way than either of these? Draw it and underneath write down how many cuts it would take altogether.

The next day Egbert buys another cake. He decides that he just cannot wait a whole hour between pieces, so he will cut it into 24 pieces and have a piece every half hour.

Draw the quickest way of cutting a cake into 24 pieces, and underneath write down how many cuts it would take altogether.

(A hard question!) Another day Egbert wanted to cut his cake into a different number of pieces. He found that the quickest way took 6 cuts. How many pieces did he want to cut it into? (There are three answers.)

4

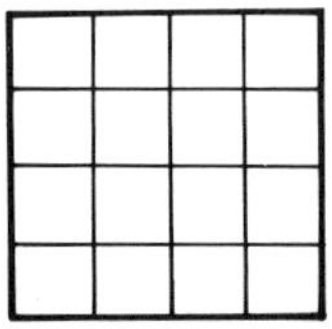

Egbert also likes chocolate, which he buys in bars of 16 pieces, like the one in the diagram opposite.

Egbert wants to take 4 pieces, and he wants to take them in one "lump". He also wants the 12 pieces left behind to be in one "lump". So he could take:

(He doesn't mind cutting them out with a knife.)

Make sketches to show as many different ways as you can of taking the 4 pieces. It is important to realise that some ways which look different from each other at first are really the same (but turned round or turned over).

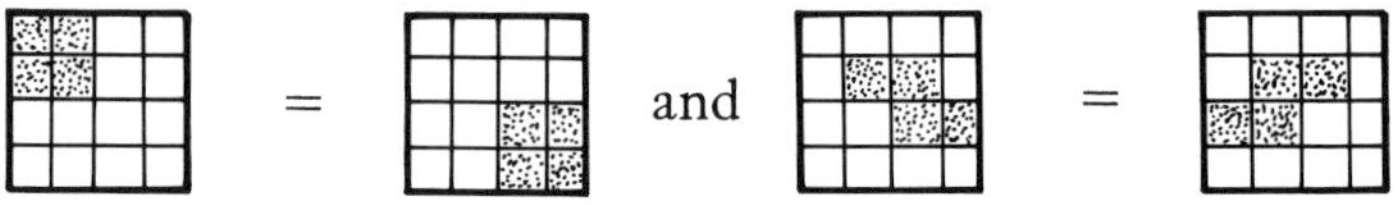

4. MEASUREMENT I

PRACTICE 1 (A)

1

Look at the diagram below and measure:

a) the length of the shortest line in millimetres

b) the length of the longest line in centimetres.

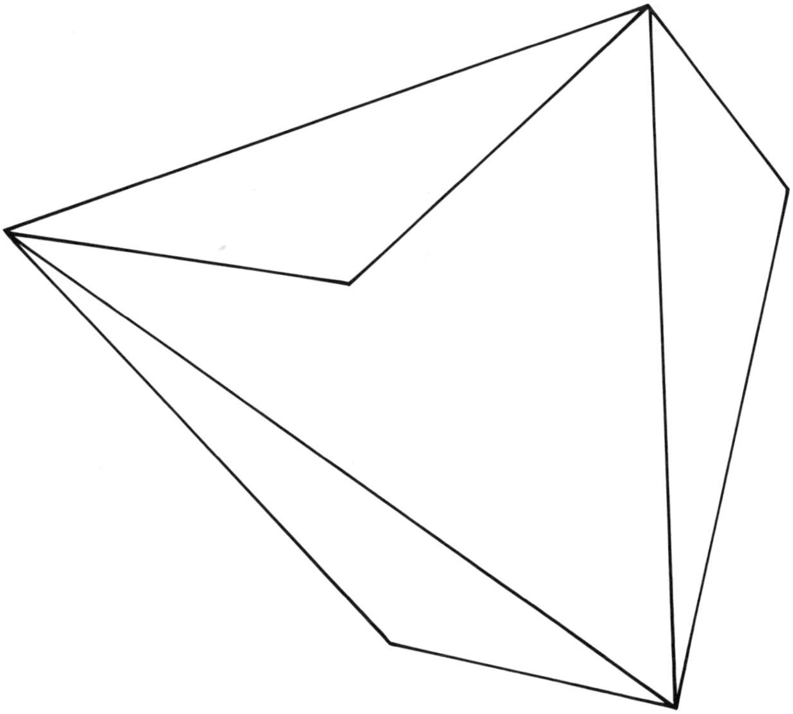

2

Use a sharp pencil for this question, and do everything really accurately – don't rush.

Draw triangles of the sizes given below, using the squares of your book to help you get a perfect right angle. Then measure the length of the third side.

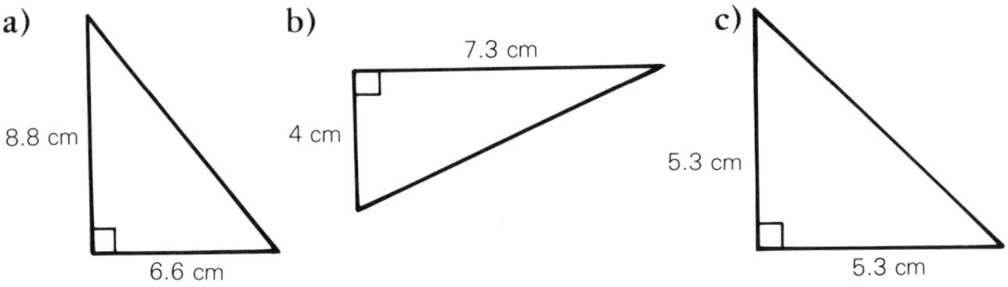

3

Copy the following questions out, putting the right number in place of the question mark:

a) 27 mm = ? cm

b) 4.5 m = ? cm

c) 6.5 cm = ? mm

d) 600 mm = ? cm

e) 60 cm = ? m

f) 1 m = ? mm

4

Emma finds that on average, if she takes 10 of her paces, she walks 6 m.

a) Find the length of 1 pace in m.

b) Find the length of 1 pace in cm.

c) Emma's garden is 30 paces long. How many metres long is the garden?

d) It is 300 m from the Science Lab to the Dining Hall. How many paces would it take Emma to walk it?

5

Guess sensibly:

a) the length of a bus in metres

b) the length of a £1 note in centimetres

c) the length of a grain of rice in millimetres.

6

a) A maths exercise book is 4 mm thick. Mr Abel, the maths teacher, has a pile of books 14 cm high, waiting to be marked. How many books is this? (**Hint**: how many mm is 14 cm?)

b) The school football pitch is 30 m wide and 45 m long. If I run round it 10 times, how far will I have run in metres? How far in kilometres?

7

You have some sticks which are 4 cm long, 6 cm long and 11 cm long – lots of each size, so you are not going to run out.

You could make a length of 23 cm like this:

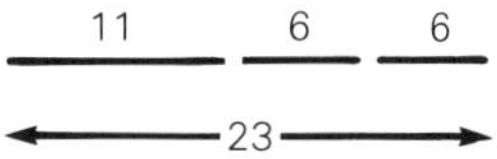

You could make a length of 13 cm like this:

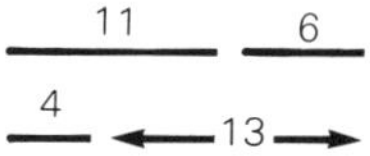

Draw diagrams like the ones above to show how you could make the following lengths, using as few sticks as possible:

a) 25 cm b) 40 cm c) 3 cm d) 16 cm e) 1 m

f) How could you use 7 sticks precisely to make a length of 2 cm?

PRACTICE 2 (BCD)

1

Turn these a.m./p.m. times to 24-hour clock times:

a) 7.15 a.m. b) 5.30 p.m. c) 11.25 p.m. d) 12.30 a.m.

Turn these 24 hour clock times to a.m./p.m. times:

e) 0530 f) 1945 g) 2200 h) 0045

2

How many:

a) days in March, April and May put together

b) seconds in $3\frac{1}{2}$ minutes

c) weeks in 105 days

d) hours and minutes in 320 minutes

e) days has Angus been alive if it is his 11th birthday today – don't worry about leap years

f) leap years are there between 1982 and 1999

g) 20-minute music lessons can a teacher fit into 4 hours with no gaps between lessons

h) years and months is 39 months?

3

a) A 3-minute phone call costs 5 p. How much would it cost to phone for 45 minutes?

b) A film starts at 1915 and finishes at 2130. How many minutes does it last?

c) John is 12 years 9 months, Susan is 11 years 7 months and David is 9 years 4 months. What do their three ages add up to?

4

The timetable opposite shows the bus service from Mudtown to Deadend village. Some of the buses pass through one or both of the villages of Much Snoring and Loose Chippings. The fast buses go directly from Mudtown to Deadend without stopping.

Mudtown	0715	0750	0830	0925	0955	1400	1620	1950
Much Snoring	0732	0807	–	0942	–	1417	1637	–
Loose Chippings	–	0831	–	1006	–	1441	–	–
Deadend	0805	0848	0907	1023	1032	1458	1710	2027

a) I have to take a bus from Loose Chippings to Deadend. What is the earliest time I can get to Deadend in the morning?

b) How long does it take a fast bus to travel from Mudtown to Deadend?

c) At what times during the day are there buses from Much Snoring?

d) How long does it take a bus to get from Mudtown to Much Snoring?

e) On Fridays I finish work at 3 o'clock in the afternoon. At what time does the next bus after that leave Mudtown for Deadend?

f) In Deadend it takes at least 5 minutes to walk from the bus stop to the railway station. I have to get the bus from Mudtown to Deadend, then catch the 1034 train from Deadend to London. Which bus should I catch from Mudtown?

5

a) A boy can walk 600 metres in 8 minutes. What is his speed in m/min?

b) A car travels 8 km in 5 minutes. How far would it travel in 1 hour (60 minutes) at this speed?

c) Another car travels 390 km in 6 hours. What is its speed in km/h?

d) A snail in a hurry crawls 6 metres in 8 minutes. What is its speed in cm/min?

e) I can walk at a steady 6 km/h. How long will it take me to walk 18 km? How long will it take me to walk 27 km?

f) A steady running speed is 5 m/s. At this speed:

(i) How many metres could I run in a minute?

(ii) How many metres could I run in an hour?

(iii) How many kilometres could I run in an hour?

SUMMARY

1

The map below shows the roads and villages around where Tom lives. It also shows the distance between villages in kilometres.

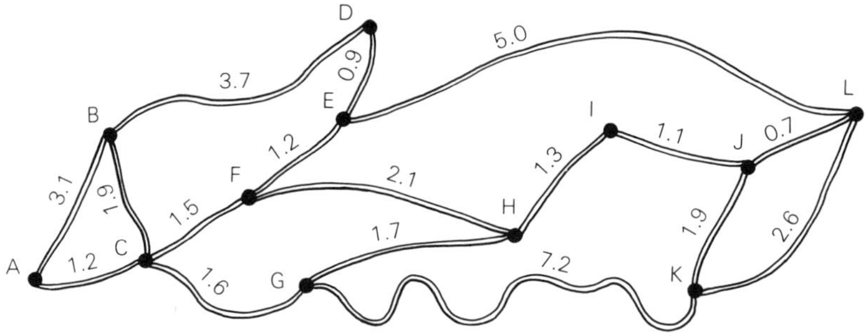

a) Tom wants to cycle from A to L. There are several ways he could take: one way would be A to B to D to E to L, which is a total distance of 12.7 km. Which is the shortest way, and how many kilometres is it?

b) Which villages are less than 4 km from F?

c) One day, Tom's father has to leave their house in J to visit people in E, K, L and B, then return home to J. Find his shortest route (write it down as you did in question (a)), and say how many kilometres it is.

d) Even by the shortest route, Tom's best friend lives 5.7 km from J. Which village could he live in?

2

A 1 p piece is 2 cm across. If £1 worth of pennies were laid in a line, how long would the line be? Give your answer:

a) in cm b) in m.

c) To raise money the Save the Children Fund tries to collect enough pennies to make a line 1 km long. How much would all the pennies be worth? (Use your answer to (b) to help you.)

3

Copy the questions below, putting the right number in place of the question mark:

a) 12.3 cm = ? mm b) 650 cm = ? m

c) 6.3 km = ? m d) 320 m = ? km

4

a) It is 560 m from my house to the shop. If I walk, it takes me 7 minutes, but if I run it only takes 4 minutes.

(i) What is my walking speed in m/min?

(ii) What is my running speed in m/min?

b) Emma's favourite film ("The Return of Dracula's Great-grandmother") is on television tonight, starting at 1945. The film lasts for 1 hour 50 minutes. When will it finish?

c) Some of the children from Subset House are going on a school trip to France. They leave very early on June 28th and get back late on July 3rd. How many days are they away from school?

5

In a certain game you have to run from a tree, T, touch the wall and then carry on to a post, P.

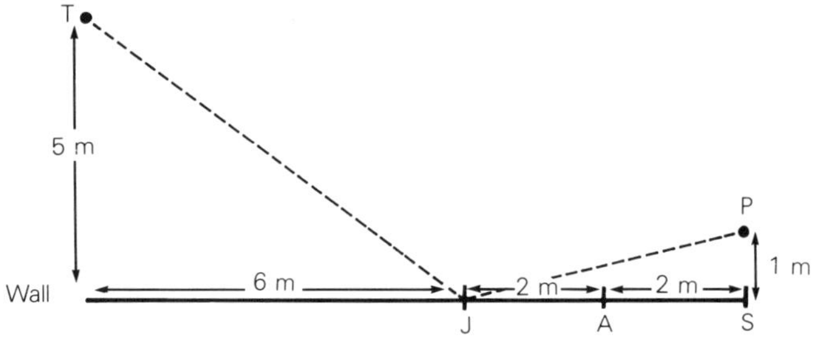

John decides to touch the wall at J; Anne thinks A is the best place; and Sarah chooses S. (John's run is shown in the diagram.)

Being as careful and accurate as you can, make a drawing using cm instead of m. By careful measuring find out which of the three children has the shortest run. How long is the shortest run? *Note*: the wall is 10 m long altogether.

1

When Mr Abel, the maths teacher, is in a good mood, his pace is 60 cm long, but when he's in a temper it increases to 80 cm.

a) When he's in a good mood, it takes Mr Abel 20 paces to cross the dining hall. How far is it across the dining hall in metres? How many paces would it take him when he's in a temper?

b) Mr Abel was furious to see Tom and Emma climbing trees in their best clothes. He strode across the field to tell them off, and it took him 20 paces less than it would have done if he had been in a good mood. How far away were the children when he spotted them? (Use your answer to (a) to help you.)

c) When he is confused Mr Abel takes one of his long paces, then one of his short paces, then a long, then a short, and so on. How many paces would it take him to cover 7 m when he is confused?

2

Mr and Mrs Meeter have an annoying daughter called Milly who likes to confuse people by using awkward units. For instance she will say that her pigtail is 0.0006 km long, or that she lives 4 500 000 mm from school.

Complete:

a) 0.0006 km = ? m = ? cm

b) 4 500 000 mm = ? cm = ? m = ? km

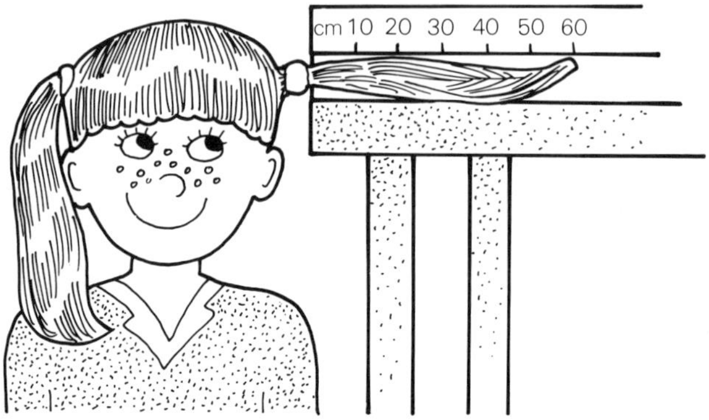

3

Professor Mildew likes his breakfast boiled egg runny – cooked for 3 minutes to be precise. Mrs Mildew likes hers hard – cooked for 5 minutes. To solve this problem they have two eggtimers: one which times 3 minutes, and another which times 5 minutes.

The trouble starts when Aunt Beatrice comes to stay, for she likes hers cooked for 4 minutes. "If only she wanted it done for 8 minutes, then it would be easy," said the professor. "All I would have to do is:

> put the egg in and set the 3 minute timer going at the same time. When the 3 minute timer finishes, immediately set the 5 minute one going. When that finishes, take the egg out. Result: 8 minutes precisely.

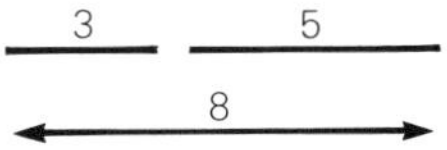

It would be just as easy to time 2 minutes, like this:

> set the 3 minute and the 5 minute timers going at the same moment. When the 3 minute is finished, immediately put the egg in. Then when the 5 minute timer finishes, take the egg out. Result: 2 minutes."

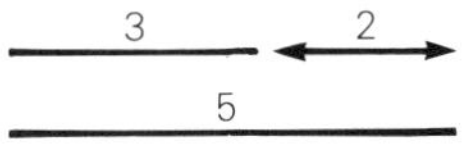

Can you find a way of using the two eggtimers to time 4 minutes? Try to describe your way with a diagram as well as in words.

How could you time 7 minutes?

5. FRACTIONS II

PRACTICE 1 (ABC)

1

Put these in order of size, starting with the smallest:

a) 0.7 $\qquad \frac{1}{2} \qquad$ 0.59 $\qquad \frac{3}{10} \qquad \frac{3}{5}$

b) 11 $\qquad$ 9.8 $\qquad 11\frac{1}{3} \qquad$ 11.5

2

Write these decimal fractions as ordinary fractions in their simplest form:

a) 0.55 $\qquad$ b) 0.40 $\qquad$ c) 0.28 $\qquad$ d) 0.06 $\qquad$ e) 0.75

3

Copy and complete the following, putting the correct number in place of the question mark:

a) $\frac{9}{20} = \frac{?}{100} = 0.?$ $\qquad$ b) $\frac{7}{50} = \frac{?}{100} = 0.?$

4

Just write down the answers to these:

a) $12.5 \div 10$ $\qquad$ b) $25.6 \div 100$ $\qquad$ c) $57 \div 10$

d) $6.02 \div 10$ $\qquad$ e) $560 \div 10$ $\qquad$ f) $280 \div 100$

5

There are exactly 100 squares in the diagram on the next page.

a) What fraction of the squares have a cross in them? Give your answer:
   (i) as a decimal fraction
   (ii) as an ordinary fraction in its simplest form.

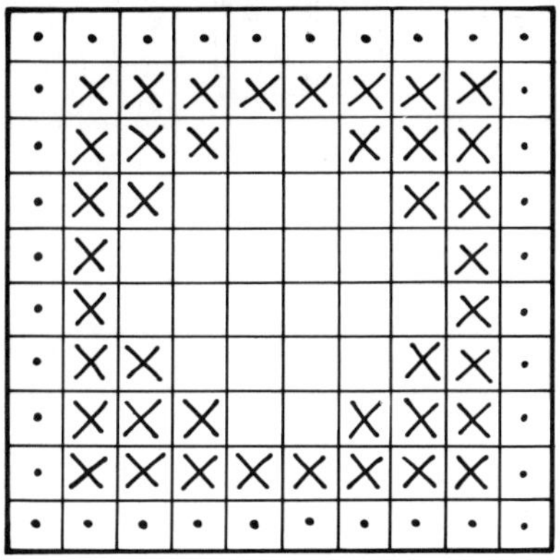

b) What fraction of the squares *aren't* on the edge of the diagram? To help you see what is meant, the edge squares contain a dot. Again, give your answer:
   (i) as a decimal fraction
   (ii) as an ordinary fraction in its simplest form.

6

Work the following out. There are no remainders – they all divide exactly, though you may have to add some 0s to get them to go, as in (a) and (b).

a) $7 \div 4$ (call it $7.00 \div 4$)　　b) $3.9 \div 6$ (call it $3.90 \div 6$)

c) $12 \div 5$　　d) $13 \div 8$

7

Don't worry about the remainders at the end. What do you notice about the three answers?

a) Write $\frac{1}{7}$ as a decimal by doing this: $7\overline{)1.000\,000}$

b) Write $\frac{3}{7}$ as a decimal by doing this: $7\overline{)3.000\,000}$

c) Write $\frac{2}{7}$ as a decimal by doing this: $7\overline{)2.000\,000}$

PRACTICE 2 (DE)

1

Remembering to mark off the lengths with your compasses, draw lines of the following lengths:

a) 2.6 cm　　b) 4.4 cm　　c) 5.1 cm　　d) 9.8 cm

2

Measure, in centimetres, on the diagram below, the following lengths:

a) AB b) AC c) AD d) BC e) BD f) CD

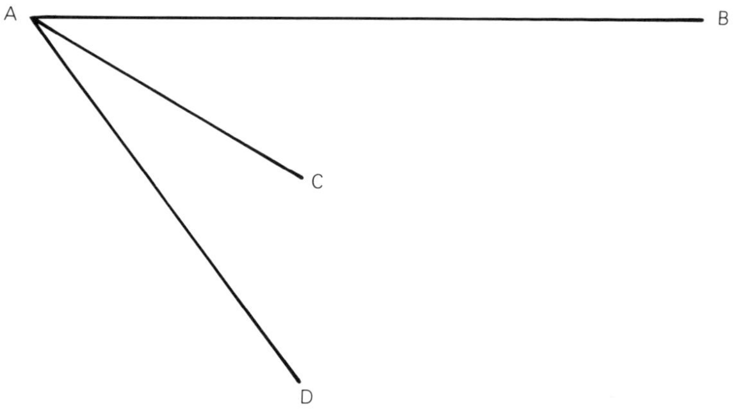

3

Fatima has just done her first long division using factors. The question was:

$$1632 \div 24$$

She did it by dividing by 3, then dividing by 8. When she finished she took it up to Mr Abel to see whether it was correct. She was pleased to find that it was!

a) Do the sum the same way Fatima did it.

As she walked back to her desk Fatima couldn't resist a quick peep over Tom's shoulder to see what he was doing. To her delight she found that he was doing the same sum, but he seemed to be doing it wrongly! He started by dividing by 4! Fatima couldn't do any more work while she waited for Tom to take his book up to be checked. But when he did, to Fatima's dismay, he also got it right.

b) Do the sum the way Tom did it.

4

Do these long divisions by factors:

a) $28\overline{)1176}$ b) $36\overline{)2088}$ c) $18\overline{)2754}$

5

Do these long divisions:

a) $17\overline{)4046}$ b) $19\overline{)7999}$ c) $35\overline{)3010}$

6

Work these out:

a) $151.2 \div 12$ b) $108.6 \div 20$ c) $31.5 \div 15$

d) $1060.8 \div 20$

SUMMARY

1

Do these divisions. They all go exactly if you put in 0s.

a) $7.5 \div 4$ b) $0.51 \div 6$ c) $0.37 \div 5$

2

a) Write as a decimal: $\frac{3}{5}$.

b) Write as a fraction in its simplest form: 0.72

3

Write down the answers to these:

a) $7.8 \div 10$ b) 0.065×10 c) $15.6 \div 100$

4

The 15 children in Form II at Subset House are going camping for the weekend. Hiring a minibus will cost £32 and the petrol will cost £16. The campsite will cost £9 for the whole group. Food will cost £1.50 per child.

How much should each child pay towards the trip?

5

Do these long divisions:

a) 34)8738   b) 25)51 200   c) 42)8232

6

Do this long division – it goes exactly.

17)9 999 999 999 999 999   (There are 16 nines.)

Can you think of a way of doing this sum on your calculator?

ALLSORTS

1

In these long divisions the stars stand for missing numbers. Work out what they are, and write out the sums as they should be.

a)
```
      2★
1★)★★★
    34
    --
     8★
     85
     --
     00
```

b)
```
      3★
★6)8★2
    ★★
    --
     ★2
     ★★
     --
     00
```

c)
```
      7★
★★)★★★6
    ★★
    --
     ★6
     ★★
     --
     00
```

2

If 124 is multipled by 59 and the answer is divided by 62, what will the result be?

3

a) Using the 13 times table on the right, work out $\frac{1}{13}$ as a decimal fraction.
The division to do is:

$$13\overline{)1.000\,000\,000\,000}$$

b) Do similar divisions (i.e. with the same number of 0s) to work out the following as decimal fractions:

13×1	=	13
13×2	=	26
13×3	=	39
13×4	=	52
13×5	=	65
13×6	=	78
13×7	=	91
13×8	=	104
13×9	=	117

$\frac{2}{13}$ $\frac{3}{13}$ $\frac{4}{13}$ $\frac{5}{13}$ $\frac{6}{13}$ $\frac{7}{13}$

$\frac{8}{13}$ $\frac{9}{13}$ $\frac{10}{13}$ $\frac{11}{13}$ $\frac{12}{13}$

c) Each division has a remainder. What happens if you add more 0s and continue dividing?

d) What else do you notice about the 12 answers?

e) Can you find other sets of ordinary fractions that form similar sets of decimal fractions?

6. GRAPHS AND FUNCTIONS I

PRACTICE 1 (ABC)

1

Look at the graph below:

A graph for converting pounds into francs

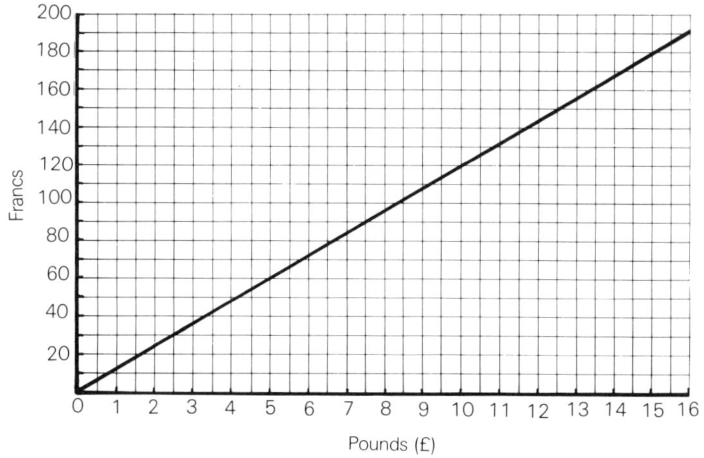

a) Tom has saved up £10.50 for the school trip to France. How many francs will he be able to change his money for?

b) Emma bought a new pair of jeans when she was in Paris. They cost her 150 francs. How much is this in pounds?

c) Turn these amounts into francs:

(i) £5.50 (ii) £15.50 (iii) £3.25

d) Turn these amounts into pounds:

(i) 85 francs (ii) 55 francs (iii) 100 francs

e) Use your last answer to turn 1000 francs into pounds.

2

1 kilogram (kg) = 2.2 pounds (lb) approximately. Copy and complete this table:

kg	0	2	4	6	8	10
lb						

Now draw axes like the ones below, but make them bigger: the kg axis should go up to 10, and the lb axis up to 25.

The short way of describing these axes is:

"1 cm to 1 kg, and 1 cm to 2 lb."

Check on your axes that each cm *does* stand for 1 kg on the horizontal axis, and for 2 lb on the vertical axis.

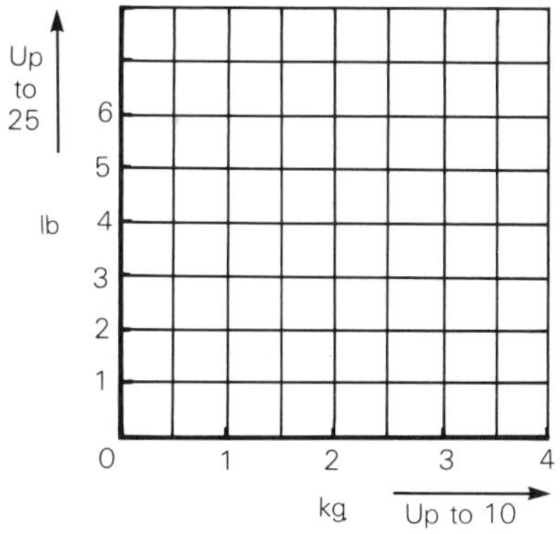

Now mark the points from your table on to your graph. Be as accurate as you can.

Finally, join up the points with a straight line. If they *don't* join up properly then check your table, and check you have put the points correctly on to your graph.

When you are certain your graph is right, answer these questions:

a) 1 stone is 14 pounds. How many kilograms is 1 stone? Give your answer as a decimal fraction.

b) Oliver found that his briefcase weighed 4.3 kg. What was its mass in pounds?

c) Turn $19\frac{1}{2}$ lb into kilograms.

3

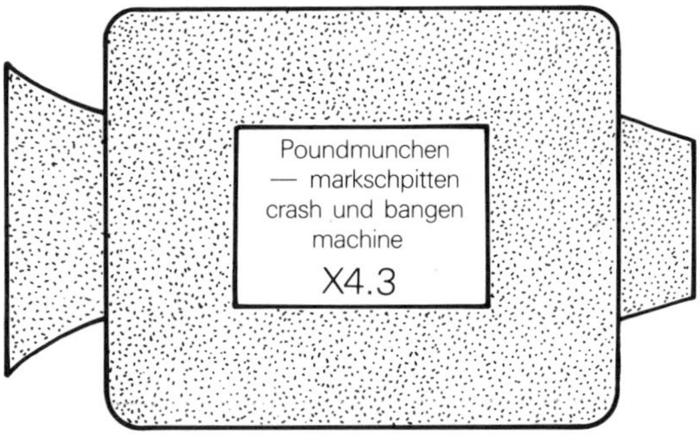

a) The machine on the right converts pounds into German marks. How many marks could I get for £5?

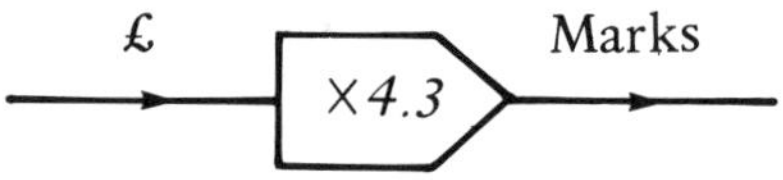

b) This machine turns kilometres into miles.

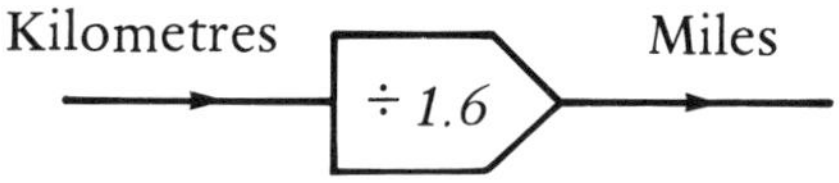

(i) How many kilometres is 1 mile? (Think carefully!)

(ii) How many miles is 16 kilometres?

c) Major Bottleneck, the famous traveller and explorer, wants to know how to convert French francs into German marks.

He knows how to convert francs into pounds:

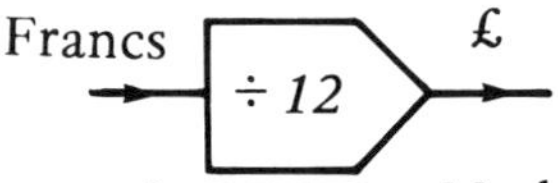

He knows how to convert pounds into marks:

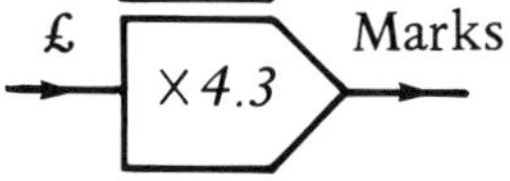

After several hours' thought, he realised that you could join the two machines together so that the pounds coming out of the francs machine went straight into the marks machine:

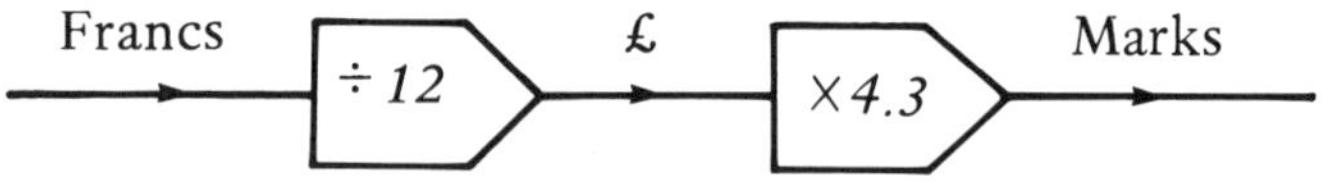

(i) Put 120 francs through the machines. How many marks come out?

(ii) It's not difficult to invent a double machine that will turn marks into francs:

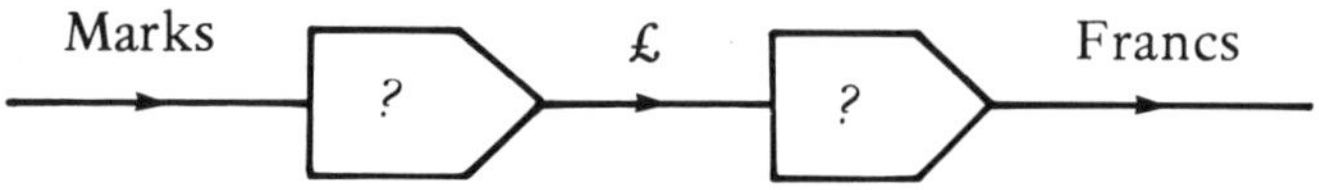

Copy the diagram above, putting the correct numbers and signs in place of the question marks.

PRACTICE 2 (CD)

1

To make a gallon of elderberry wine you need 3 pounds of sugar. This can be put into a number machine:

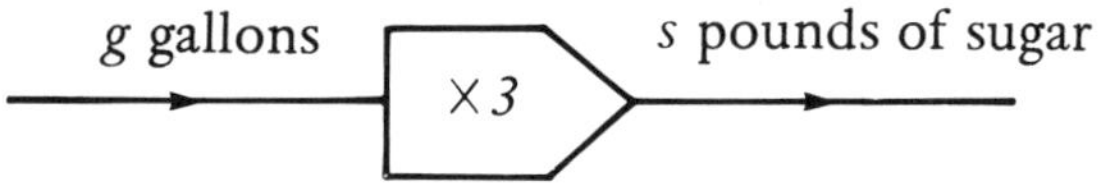

a) If the number of gallons is called g and the number of pounds of sugar is called s, make a formula:

$$s = \dots$$

b) Now make another formula:

$$g = \dots$$

2

Make formulae for these machines:

a)

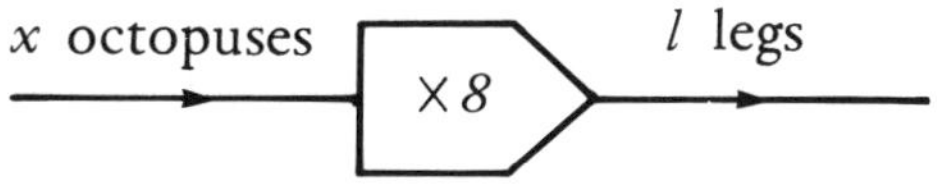

$l = \dots$

b)

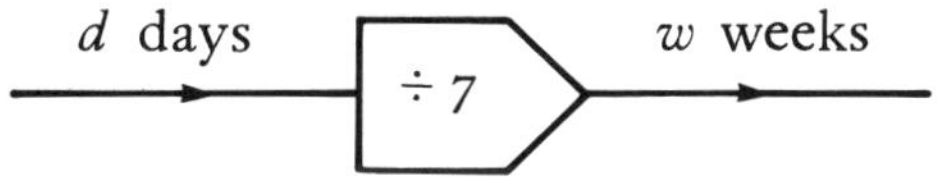

$d = \dots$

c)

$p = \dots$

3

Mr Abel, the maths teacher, never comes to school without a little black book containing graphs and formulae that enable him to work out almost anything in practically no time at all.

One of the most important of these is the homework graph. Mr Abel knows that to mark one maths homework takes $3\frac{1}{2}$ minutes. The graph shows how long it will take to mark any number of homework exercises up to 24. It uses these scales:

Horizontal: 1 cm to 2 homework exercises (going up to 24).

Vertical: 1 cm to 10 minutes (going up to 100).

a) Mark out these axes in your book.

b) Copy and complete: 0 homework exercises take . . . minutes
10 homework exercises take . . . minutes
20 homework exercises take . . . minutes

c) Mark these points on your graph. Join them up with a straight line going right across the page – don't stop short of the end of the horizontal axis. (If your 3 points are not in a straight line, check everything and find your mistake.)

Use your graph to answer these questions:

d) How many homework exercises can Mr Abel mark in an hour?

e) There are 14 children in Form IIIa and 19 children in Form IIIb. How long will it take to mark all their homework exercises? Give your answer in hours and minutes.

4

Ruritania has not yet gone metric. Their money is very confusing to tourists: the smallest coin is the wadge; there is a middle coin called a wedge; and the most valuable coin is the widge. They are connected like this:

7 wadges = 1 wedge

5 wedges = 1 widge

a) How many wadges is one widge worth?

b) Copy and complete these number machines and formulae:

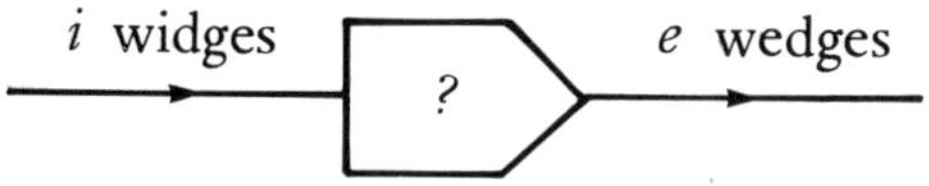

$e = \ldots$

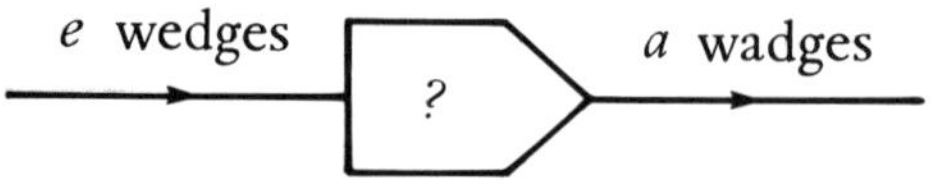

$a = \ldots$

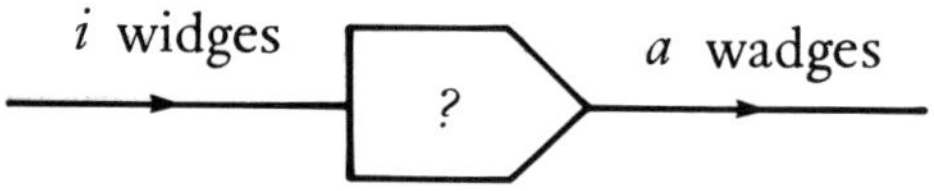

$a = \ldots$

c) A man saves all his small coins in a bottle. At the end of the year he has saved 4200 wadges.

(i) How many wedges is this?

(ii) How many widges is this?

SUMMARY

1

The graph below shows how a factory worker's wages can be calculated from the number of hours he or she works in the week. The line is not straight because anything over 40 hours counts as overtime, and is better paid (so the line gets steeper).

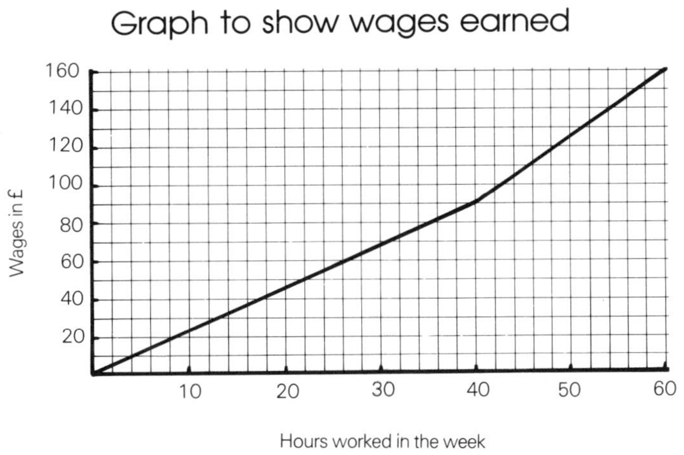

Use the graph to answer these questions:

a) How much should a worker who worked for 36 hours be paid?

b) A grommet-tightener works every day from Monday to Saturday from 0830 till 1330. What should his weekly wage be?

c) If a worker earned £110, how many hours did she work?

d) One week, Fred worked for 40 hours and Jo worked for 50 hours. How much was each paid? How much extra money did Jo get for the extra 10 hours she worked?

e) "If only I'd worked twice as long, I'd have earned £140," one man was heard to say. How much did he actually earn? (Not £70.)

2

Mr Abel, the maths teacher, calculates his children's pocket-money according to this formula: a child m months old receives p pence pocket money, where:

$$p = \frac{m}{2}$$

a) Euclid, the younger boy, is $4\frac{1}{2}$ *years* old. What is his pocket money?

b) Pythagoras gets 60 p pocket-money. How old is he? How much will he get in one year's time?

3

There are two supermarkets near my home called Ripoff and Shoddygoods. Oranges cost $5\frac{1}{2}$ p at Ripoff and $6\frac{1}{2}$ p at Shoddygoods.

Complete these two tables:

Ripoff			
Oranges bought	0	10	20
Cost (p)			

Shoddygoods			
Oranges bought	0	10	20
Cost (p)			

Now draw these axes:

Horizontal: 1 cm to 2 oranges, going up to 24 oranges.

Vertical: 1 cm to 10 p, going up to 160 p.

Finally, draw the line for Ripoff, then draw the line for Shoddygoods.

Use your graph to answer these questions:

a) How many oranges could I buy for £1 at each of the two supermarkets?

b) How much would 23 oranges cost at Shoddygoods?

c) I bought 15 oranges at Ripoff. How many oranges would I have been able to get at Shoddygoods with the same money?

4

Make formulae for these machines:

a)

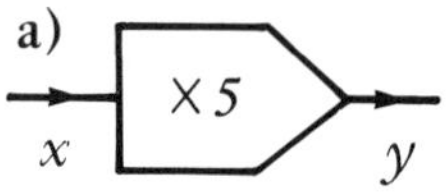

$y = \ldots$

b)

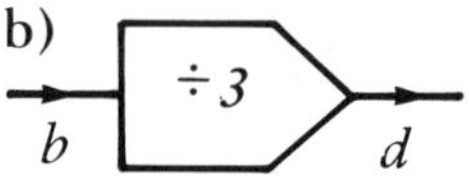

$d = \ldots$

c)

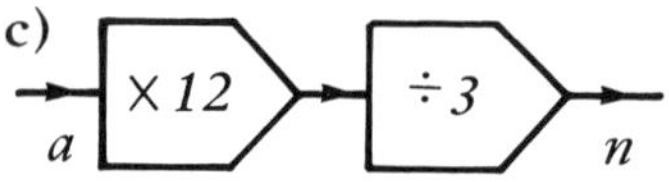

$n = \ldots$

1

Egbert is a greedy little boy, but even his stomach has its limits. Given an unlimited supply of chocolate biscuits, his progress goes like this:

For the first 5 minutes he can eat 3 biscuits each minute.

How many biscuits has he eaten in these 5 minutes?

For the next 10 minutes he can only manage 2 biscuits each minute.

How many biscuits has he eaten in these 10 minutes?

How many biscuits has he eaten in the 15 minutes since he started?

After that he can carry on at the rate of 1 biscuit each minute.

a) Copy and complete this table:

Minutes after starting	Number of biscuits eaten altogether
0	
5	
15	
25	

b) Draw axes using a horizontal scale of 1 cm to 2 minutes, and a vertical scale of 1 cm to 5 biscuits.

c) Mark on your axes the 4 points from the table. They will not line up; join them like this:

d) There are 16 biscuits in a packet. Use your graph to work out how long 2 packets would last Egbert.

e) Using your graph, or just by doing a sum, find out how long 100 biscuits would last Egbert.

2

At an apple pie factory each baker produces 500 pies in a day. Each pie is worth 30 p. 50 pies are packed into a box for delivery to shops. 20 of these boxes fit in the factory lorry. Each pie uses $\frac{1}{2}$ kg of apples and $\frac{1}{4}$ kg of flour. Flour comes to the factory in 25 kg bags.

Copy and complete these number machines:

a) Bakers working → ? → Pies produced

b) Bags of flour used → ? → Pies produced

c) Pies produced → ? → Value of pies (pence)

d) Bakers working → ? → kg of apples used

e) kg of flour used → ? → kg of apples used

f) Number of times the lorry is filled → ? → Number of pies produced

In answering these questions, it may help you to think each time: "How many pies were produced?"

g) On Monday 1500 kg of apples were used. How many bakers were working?

h) On Tuesday the lorry made 4 journeys. How much were the pies produced that day worth?

i) On Wednesday 50 bags of flour were used. How many boxes of pies were filled?

j) On Thursday 12 bakers were working, How many journeys did the lorry make?

7. ANGLES AND PARALLELS

PRACTICE 1 (AB)

1

Measure the angles marked a, b, c, d, e, f, g, h, i and j:

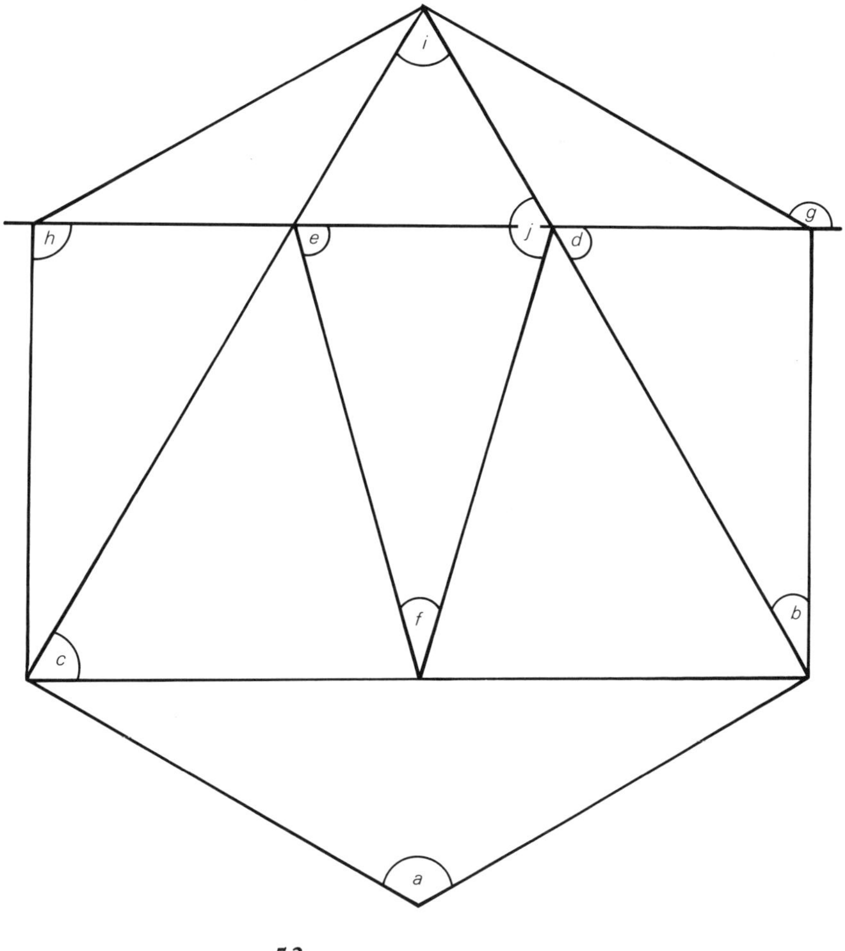

2

Calculate (don't measure) the angles marked *a*, *b*, *c*, *d*, *e*, *f*, *g*, *h*, *i* and *j*. Work in alphabetical order – it will make things easier.

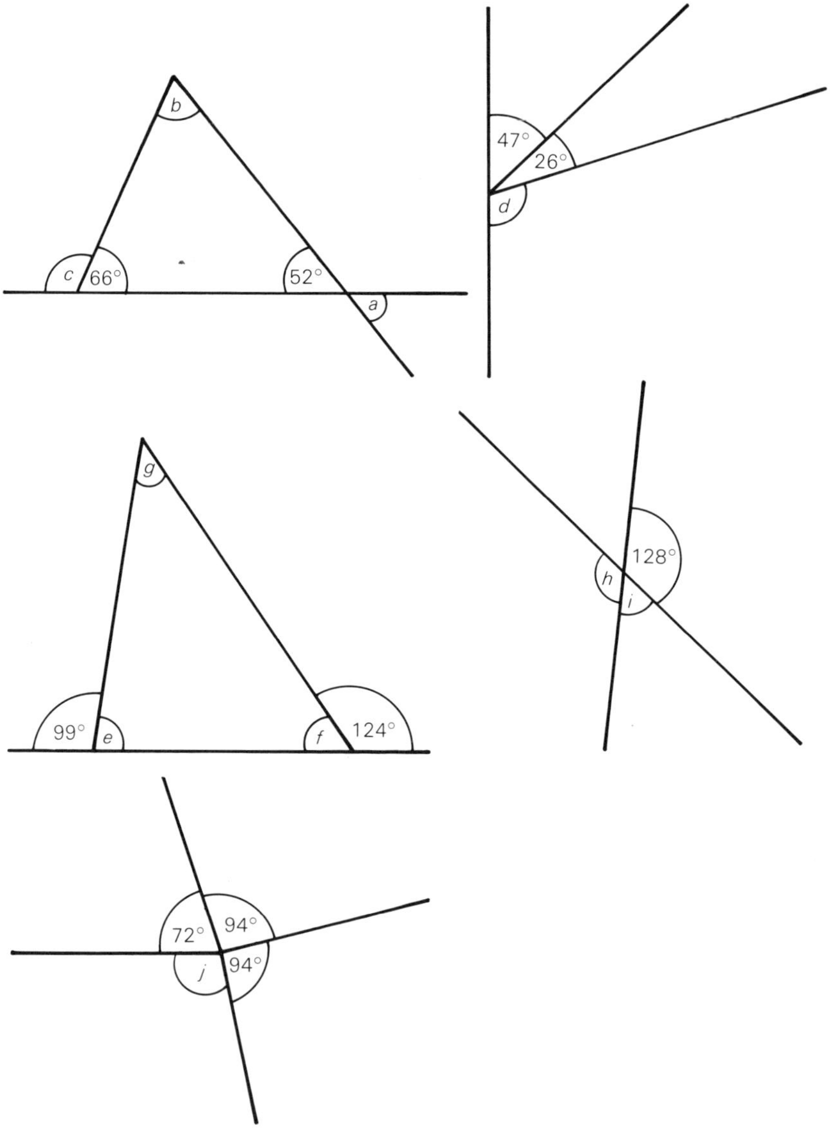

3

a) Measure the 5 angles of the pentagon on the next page. Add them up to find their total.

b) Now draw another pentagon in your book. Make it about the same size as the one on the next page. Then measure its angles and find their total.

(The total should be the same for both pentagons.)

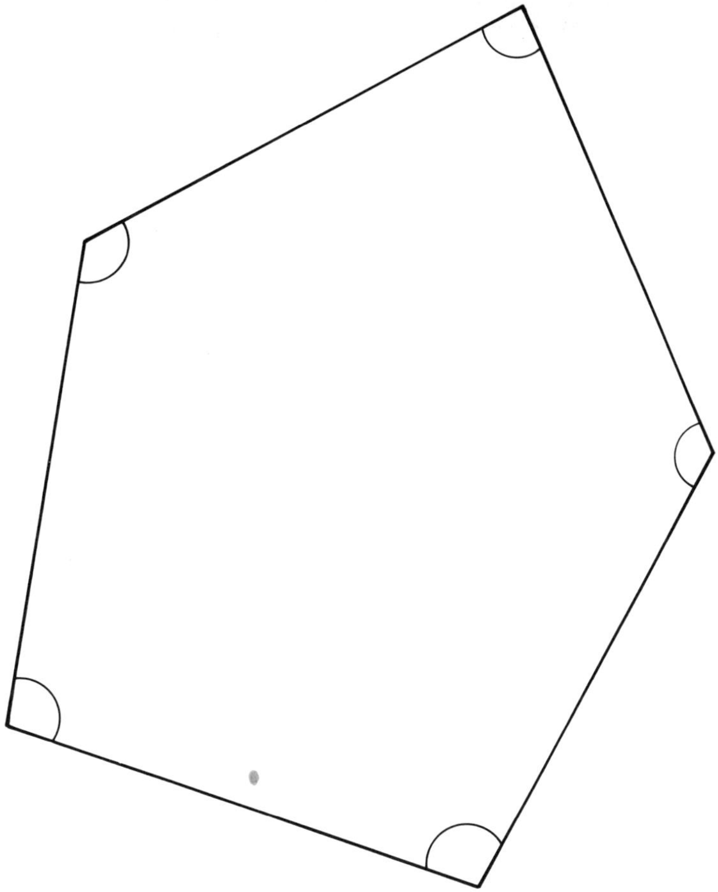

4

Calculate the angles marked a, b, c and d.

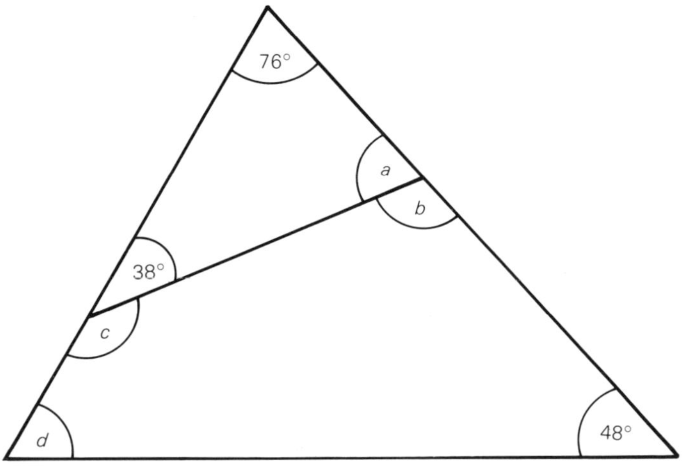

PRACTICE 2 (CD)

1

In the diagram below, a and b are *alternate* angles. You also need to be able to recognise *corresponding* and *vertically opposite* angles.

What kind of angles are:

a) a and c	**b)** b and c	**c)** g and j	**d)** g and h
e) h and d	**f)** e and b	**g)** d and f	**h)** i and k?

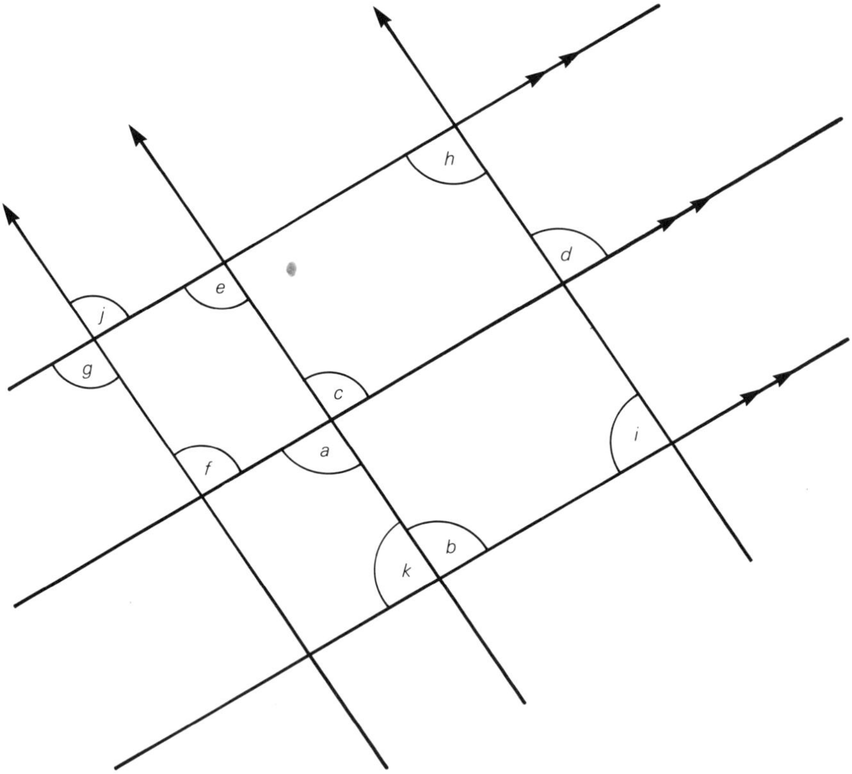

2

(A very easy question!) Make a rough copy of the diagram opposite and write in the sizes of the seven missing angles marked with a dot.

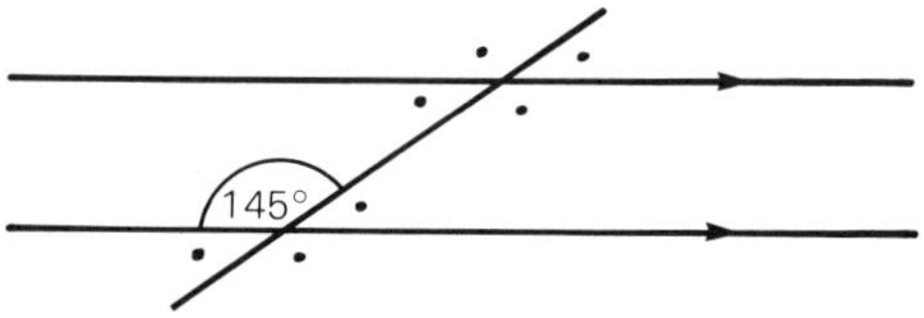

3

Find the angles marked a, b, c, d, e and f. If it helps, make a rough copy of the diagram in your book.

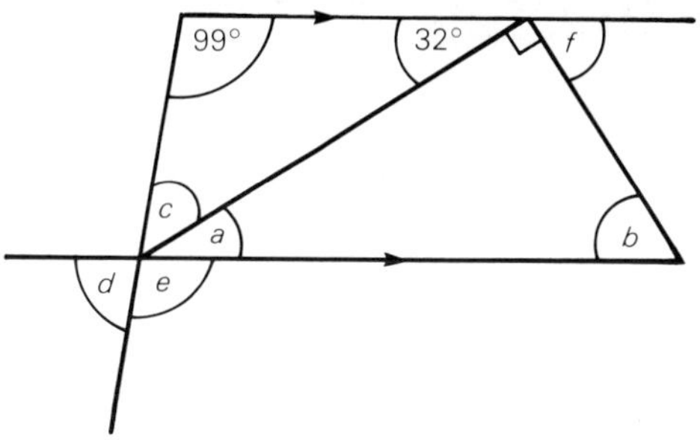

4

Find the angles marked a, b, c, d, e and f.

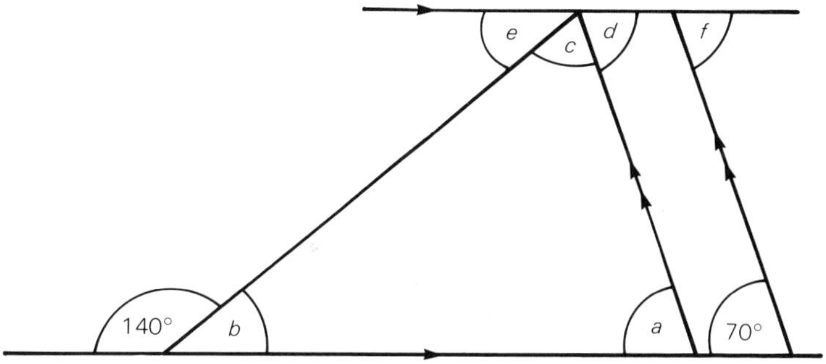

5

In the diagram below, one rectangle has been laid across another.

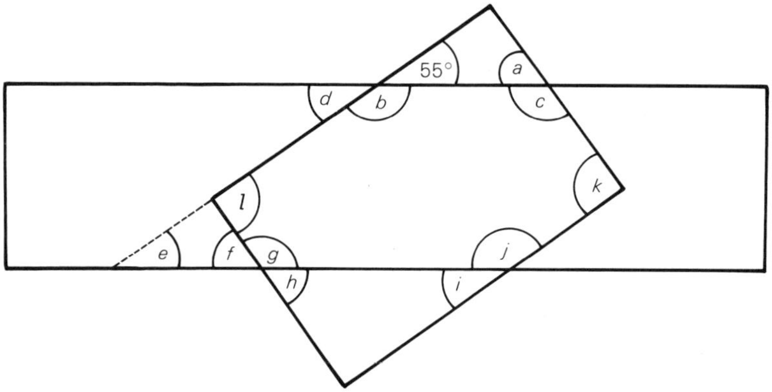

a) Calculate the angles $a, b, c, d, e, f, g, h, i, j, k$ and l.

b) Angles b, c, k, j, g and l are the angles of a hexagon. Find their sum (add them up).

SUMMARY

1

Calculate each of the angles marked from *a* to *o* in the diagram below.

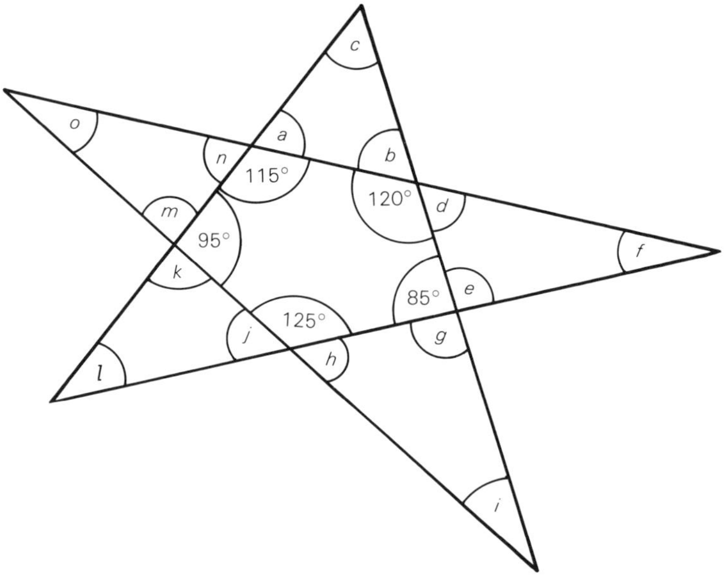

Add up angles c, f, i, l and o (the angles at the points of the "star").

2

Make a rough copy of the diagram below. (Draw the two pairs of parallel lines first, then put the last line in.)

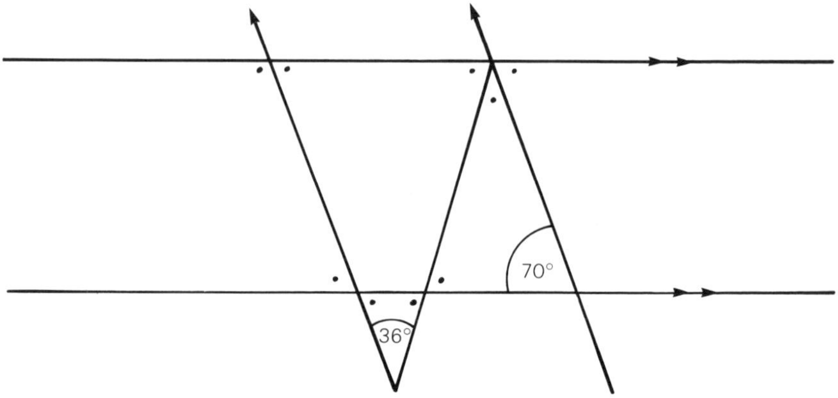

Now write in the sizes of the angles marked with a dot.

3

Angles greater than 180° are called *reflex* angles. Calculate the values of the reflex angles a, b, c and d in the following:

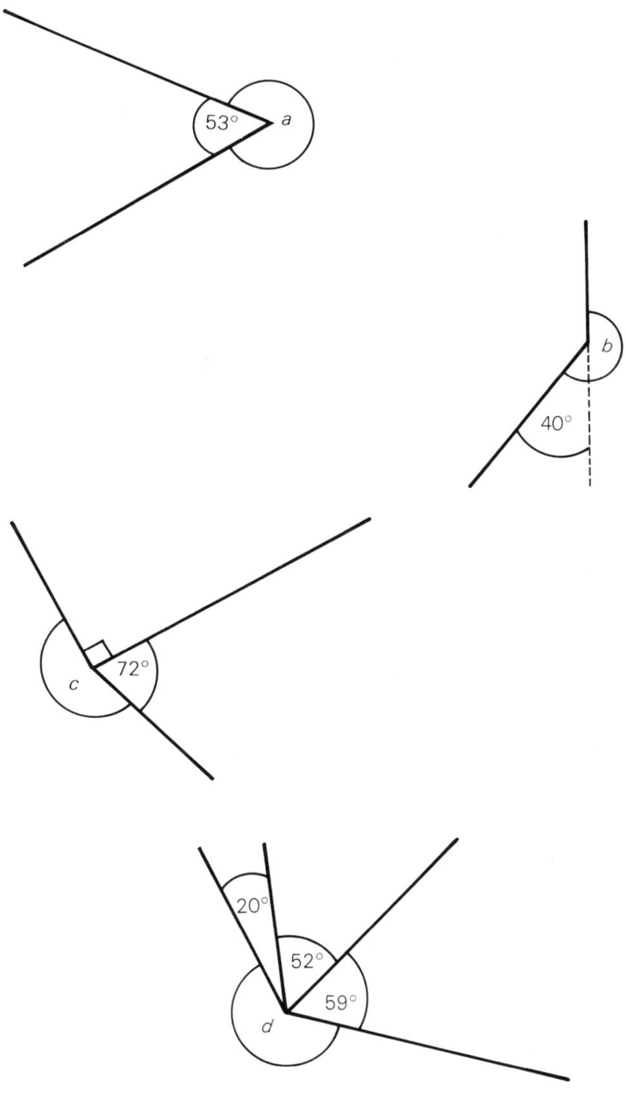

4

a) In a certain triangle, the largest angle is 3 times the size of the middle angle, and the middle angle is double the smallest angle. Find the smallest angle.

b) How many triangles can be drawn using only these angles:

$$20°, 30°, 40°, 50°, 60°, 100°, 110°, 120°, 130°?$$

For example, 40°, 40°, 100° is one triangle. In fact, there are 7 others.

ALLSORTS

1

Look at this list of shapes:

Kite	Rhombus	Pentagon
Triangle	Hexagon	Parallelogram
Trapezium	Regular hexagon	Regular pentagon

Some of these shapes *must* have two parallel sides included in them. Others *may or may not* have two parallel sides, just depending how they are drawn, while others *can't* ever have two parallel sides.

Make column headings like the ones below, and put each shape in the correct column.

Must *May or may not* *Can't*

2

The diagrams below show angles from various regular polygons.

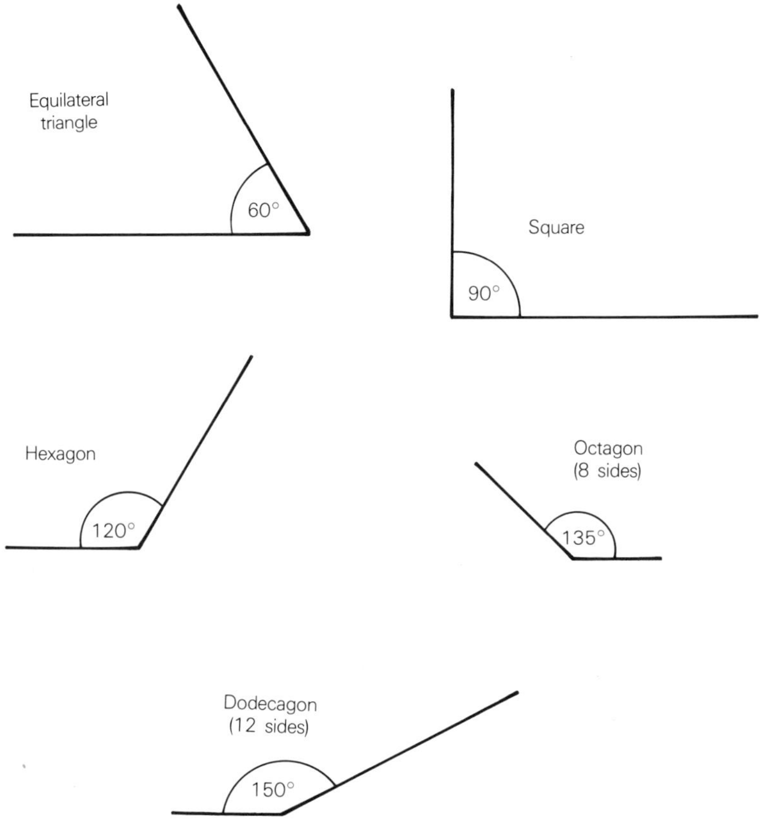

A square, a hexagon and a dodecagon would fit together without leaving any gap because their angles add up to 360°:

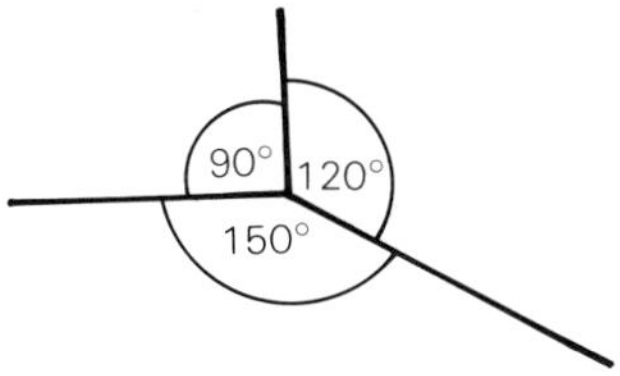

Three equilateral triangles and two squares would also fit together without leaving a gap; their angles add up to 360° too.

Find as many other ways as you can of fitting these regular polygons together. You don't have to draw them, just write them down.

3

This diagram hasn't been drawn exactly right. Lots of lines *look* parallel, but in fact they may be a few degrees off.

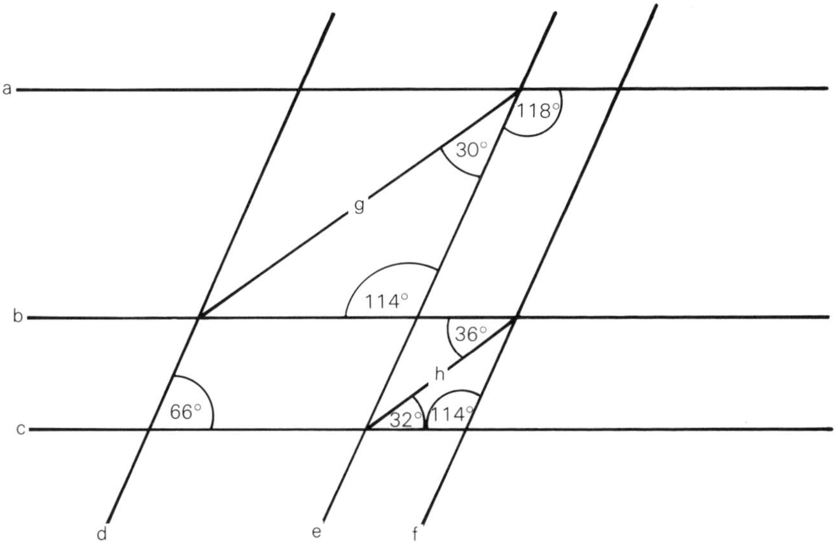

Make a rough copy of the diagram and fill in as many other angles as you can. Remember *not* to assume lines are parallel.

Now, by looking at angles, see which pairs of lines are really parallel. Remember, if lines are parallel then alternate and corresponding angles must be equal.

8. STATISTICS I

PRACTICE 1 (AB)

1

This pictogram shows the weekly pocket-money of 5 children in a family:

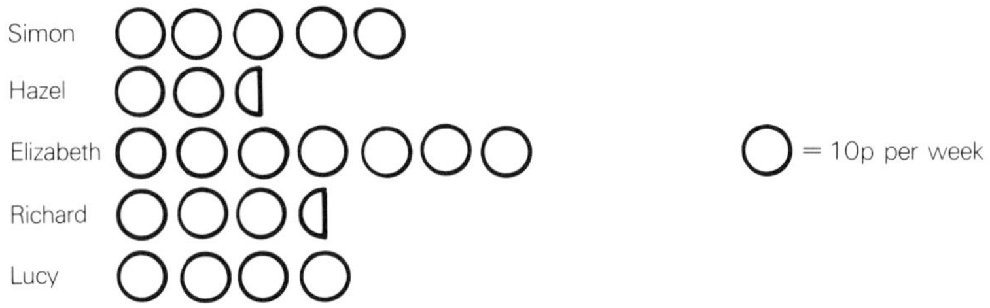

a) For how many weeks would Lucy have to save all her pocket-money in order to have at least £3?

b) How much pocket-money do the 5 children get altogether in a week?

c) In fact the children get 5 p a week for each year old they are. How old is Elizabeth?

d) How many years will it be until Richard gets 50 p a week?

2

The children in a form were asked which of the following foods they liked best: sausage, fried egg, baked beans, mushrooms. 7 said sausage, 3 said fried egg, 5 said baked beans and 2 said mushrooms.

Draw a bar chart to show these figures.

3

The pictogram on the next page shows the prices a certain firm charges per adult for a 14-day holiday in various countries:

Spain	£ £ £ £
Greece	£ £ £ £ £
Tunisia	£ £ £ £ £
Egypt	£ £ £ £ £ £ £ £
USA	£ £ £ £ £ £ £
Scotland	£ £ £
India	£ £ £ £ £ £ £ £ £ £ £

a) If the holiday in Scotland costs £150, how much does each £ stand for in the pictogram?

b) Mr Delta has at most £1000 to spend on a holiday for himself, his wife and his mother. Which of the countries can't he afford to go to with them?

c) Children travel half-price. How much would it cost a family of 2 adults and 3 children to go for a holiday in Tunisia?

d) A family of 2 adults and 2 children spent £600 on their holiday. Where did they go?

4

Here are the marks out of 10 awarded to the various children in a form:

5, 8, 2, 3, 4, 10, 6, 7, 2, 5, 5, 8, 6, 5, 8, 4, 10, 5, 8, 2.

a) Count up how many children there are in the form.

b) Draw a pictogram to show how many children got each mark. Your pictogram will start off like this:

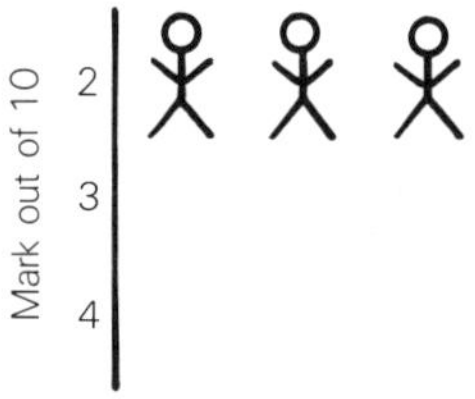

When you have finished, check that the total number of children in your pictogram is the same as your answer to (a).

PRACTICE 2 (CD)

1

18 children were asked to name their favourite lesson at school. The results are shown in the pie chart on the next page.

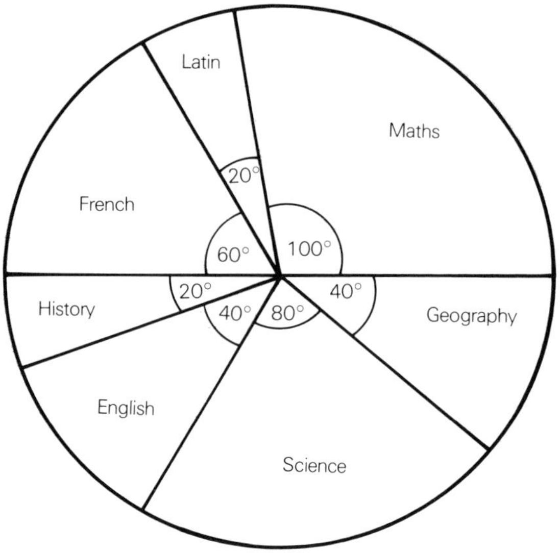

Children's favourite subjects

a) Remembering that there were 18 children in the survey, how many degrees of the circle does each child account for?

b) Use your answer to (a) to write down how many children had as their favourite subject:

(i) Maths
(ii) French
(iii) Science.

2

In the Republic of Mania there are only 3 political parties: the Communists, the Fascists and the Anarchists. When 30 typical Maniacs were asked which party they supported, the results were as follows:

Communists	14
Fascists	11
Anarchists	5

a) Remembering that there were 30 Maniacs in the survey, how many degrees of the circle should each Maniac get?

b) Now work out how many degrees should be given to the Communists, how many to the Fascists and how many to the Anarchists.

c) Finally, draw a pie chart to illustrate the figures.

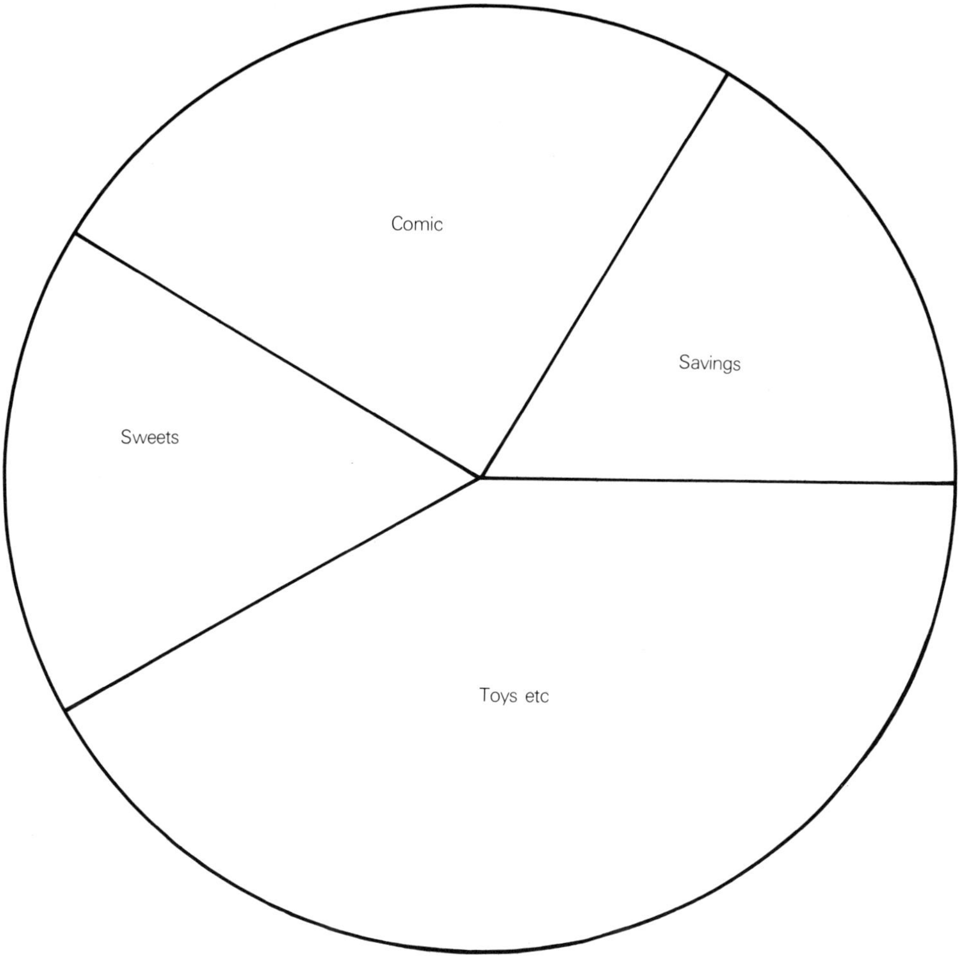

Pocket-money chart

3

The pie chart above shows how a girl spent her 60 p pocket-money one week.

a) In the pie chart how many degrees are given to each 1 p spent?

b) Use your Geoliner or protractor to measure the angles of each sector, and then copy and complete the table below. *All the amounts come out "nicely" to whole numbers of pence.*

	Degrees in pie chart	**Amount spent (pence)**
Comic	90°	
Toys		
Sweets		
Savings		

4

The table below shows how much time was given to different types of programme on a certain television channel between 4 o'clock one afternoon and 1 o'clock the next morning (when the channel closed down).

Type of programme	Time given (hours)
Films and plays	$2\frac{1}{2}$
News and documentaries	3
Comedy	$\frac{3}{4}$
Children's programmes	1
Sport	$1\frac{3}{4}$

a) What was the total number of hours included in the survey?

b) How many degrees should be given to each hour?

c) Draw a pie chart to illustrate the figures in the table.

SUMMARY

1

Pupils in the top form at Subset House School do 40 lessons a week:

Maths	8
English Subjects	14
Languages	11
Science	4
Others	3

a) Draw a pictogram to illustrate these figures.

b) Draw a bar chart to illustrate these figures.

c) Draw a pie chart to illustrate these figures.

2

The pictogram below shows how many bananas were exported by the Republic of Mania in the last few years:

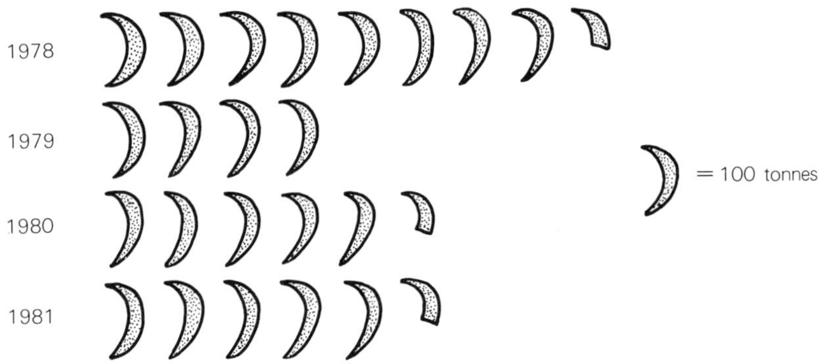

a) Write down how many tonnes of bananas you think were exported in each of the 4 years.

b) In 1978 a tonne of bananas was worth £300, while in 1981 a tonne of bananas was worth £400. In which of these 2 years was the banana crop worth more?

3

Some people might say that the lunches at Subset House School are rather monotonous. Egbert, who is very fussy about his food, kept a record for the first 40 days of term, and these were the results:

Cottage Pie	23 times
Shepherds Pie	11 times
Mince and Potatoes	6 times

Draw a pie chart to illustrate these unappetising figures.

1

Milly, just to be awkward, has invented square pie charts. Here is an example, showing the favourite sport of the 12 girls in her class:

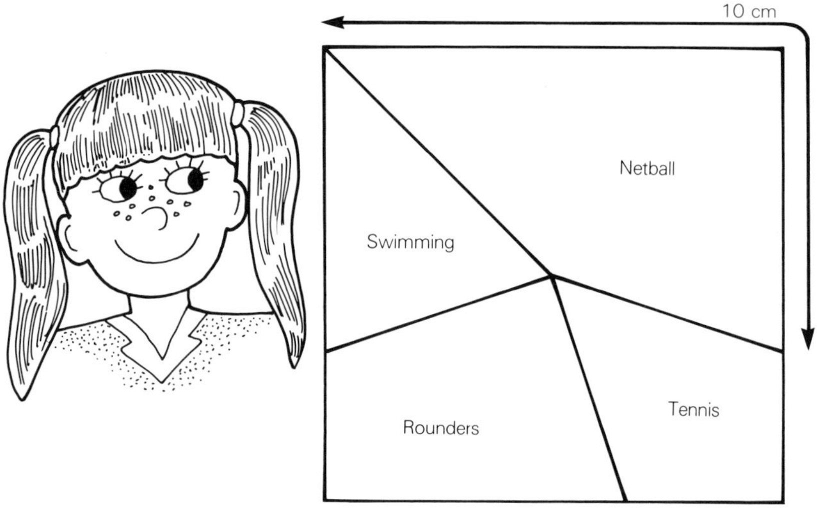

In Milly's square pie charts, it is not the angle that matters but the length of the outside of each sector.

a) The whole perimeter of the square is 24 cm (check this with your ruler). This 24 cm stands for all girls. The outside length of the netball sector is 10 cm (check this). How many girls had netball as their favourite sport?

b) How many girls had swimming, tennis and rounders as their favourite sports?

2

Dogginosh, the well-known pet food manufacturers, have just done a survey to find out which of their three new flavours dogs prefer. The three flavours were pâté de foie, gerbil and semolina, and 100 dogs were interviewed.

At the end of the survey a large pictogram was made of the results. Unfortunately Odif, a rather backward dog, preferred the flavour of the paper it was drawn on to any of the dog-food flavours, and ate part of the pictogram without anyone noticing. The only bit that was rescued was this:

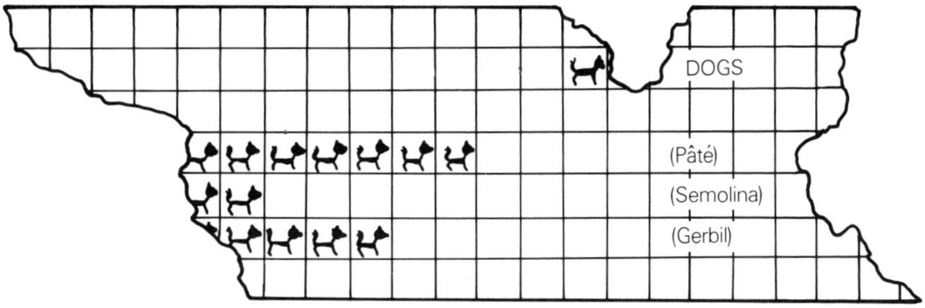

As you can see, the beginning of each row of dog pictures has been bitten off. So has the bit telling you how many dogs each picture stands for.

The only thing anyone can remember is that the number of dogs preferring pâté was 25 more than the number preferring semolina.

Can you draw a correct, new pictogram? (Remember, there were 100 dogs altogether in the survey.)

3

This pictogram shows what kind of books Tom has on his bookshelves:

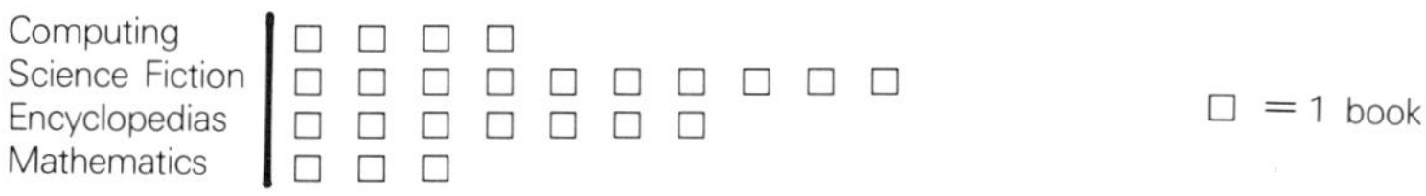

Use the pictogram to draw **a)** a bar chart and **b)** a pie chart, showing the same information.

9. GRAPHS AND FUNCTIONS II

PRACTICE 1 (AB)

1

Look at the diagram and answer the questions below.

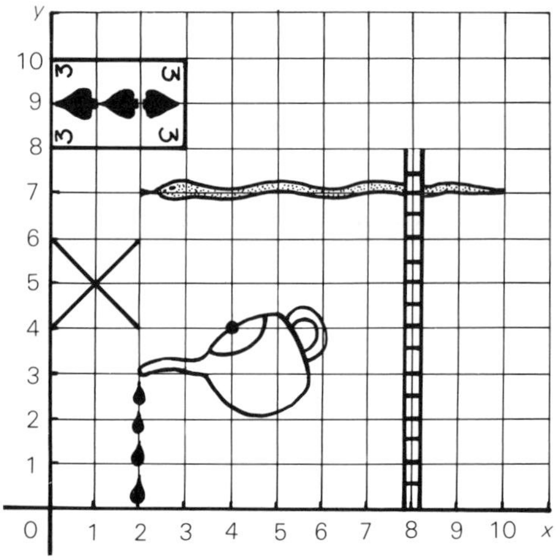

Give the coordinates of:

a) the tip of the snake's tongue.

b) the centre of the X

c) the knob on the lid of the teapot

d) the end of the teapot's spout

e) the four corners of the playing card.

Give the equation of the line:

f) the snake is lying on

g) the ladder is leaning up

h) along the top of the playing card

i) the tea is dripping down.

2

Draw axes in your book just like the ones in the diagram on p. 70.

Now join:

a) (3, 5) to (5, 7) to (3, 9) to (1, 7) and back to (3, 5)

b) (4, 2) to (5, 3) to (4, 4) to (1, 3) and back to (4, 2)

c) (5, 1) to (7, 1) to (9, 5) to (7, 5) and back to (5, 1)

d) (7, 6) to (8, 6) to (9, 7) to (9, 8) to (8, 9) to (7, 9) to (6, 8) to (6, 7) and back to (7, 6).

Put the name inside each shape – you will have to use small writing.

e) Draw the longer diagonal of shape (b). What is its equation?

f) Draw the shorter diagonal of shape (c). What is its equation?

3

Draw axes in your book like the ones in Question 1.

Now draw these lines, putting the letter beside each line:

a) $x = 6$ b) $y = 3$ c) $y = 6$ d) $x = 9$

Use your graph to solve this problem. Odif is a backward dog, but well-trained (mathematically, anyway). He distinctly remembers burying a bone somewhere. It was above the line $y = 3$ and it was below the line $y = 6$. It was to the left of the line $x = 9$ and to the right of the line $x = 6$. The coordinates were both whole numbers, and the spot definitely wasn't actually *on* any of the lines.

What are the coordinates of the points Odif should dig at?

4

Give the equations of the lines joining

a) A to E.

b) A to F.

c) A to B.

d) Give the coordinates of the middle of the line joining E to D.

e) A line is drawn from D to A and carried on beyond A. What are the coordinates of the point where this line crosses the x axis?

f) The coordinates of the point X are whole numbers, and X is exactly the same distance from C as it is from D. Give one possible pair of coordinates for X.

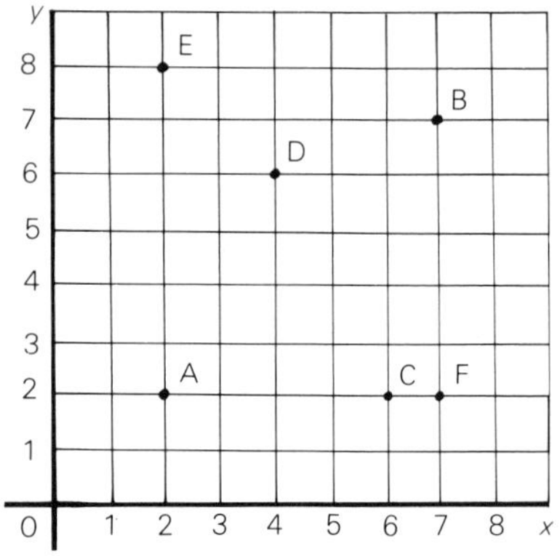

PRACTICE 2 (CD)

1

What do the letters a, b, c and so on stand for in these number machines?

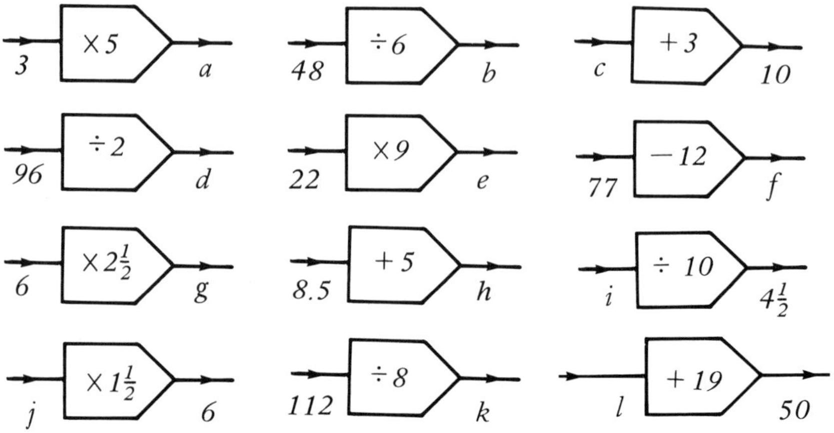

2

What do the letters a, b, c and so on stand for in these number machines?

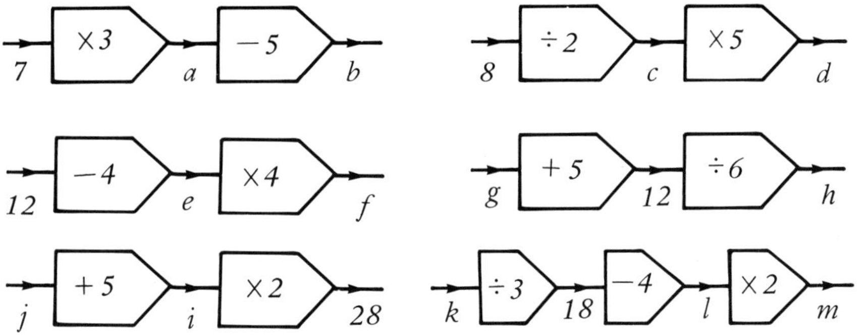

3

Copy and complete these three tables:

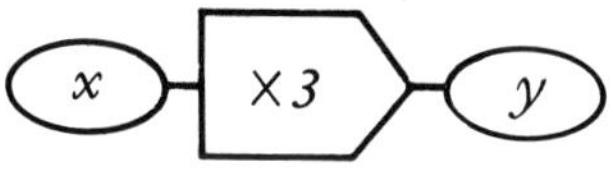

0
2
4
5

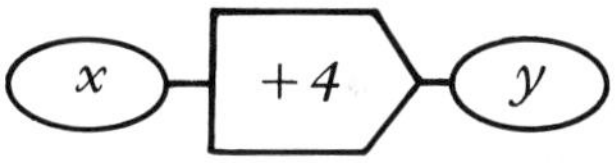

0
3
6
8
10

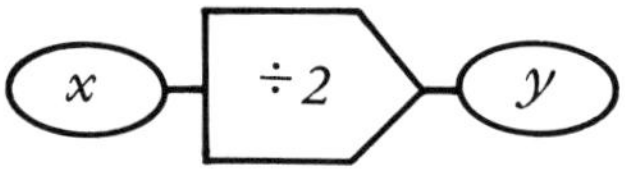

0
4
8
12

Now draw axes with x and y both going from 0 to 15. Put the points from the tables on to your graph and draw the lines through them. Do the lines one at a time, otherwise you may get muddled about which points belong to which line.

Write the equation beside each line.

4

When there is a school outing Mrs Haddock, the school cook, has a magic formula for working out how many sandwiches to make. She multiplies the number of children by 4, and adds on 10 for good luck.

The maths teacher, Mr Abel, explained to her that this could easily be done accurately with number machines. He even managed to get the handyman to convert an old potato-peeling gadget and a gramophone into the right machine:

a) Copy the diagram above, and write in what the two machines should do. Underneath it write the equation.

"You just put the children in this end and the sandwiches come out at that end," explained Mr Abel.

"Lawkes-a-mussy!" cried Mrs Haddock. "Won't the poor little mites get hurt? And where do I put the bread and butter?"

"No, no, no," said Mr Abel. "It's the *number* of children and the *number* of sandwiches I'm talking about."

b) Copy and complete this table:

x (children)	y (sandwiches)
5	
10	
20	

c) Now take a new page and draw axes like the ones on the right, but much bigger. Make the number of children (x) go up to 25, and the number of sandwiches (y) go up to 120.

Mark the points from your table on to the graph, and draw a straight line through them.

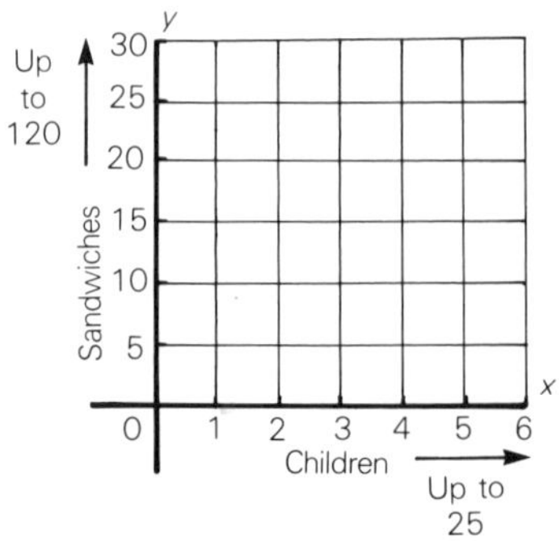

d) Last week Mrs Haddock had to cut 70 sandwiches. Use your graph to work out how many children there were on the outing.

SUMMARY

1

The map shows an island.

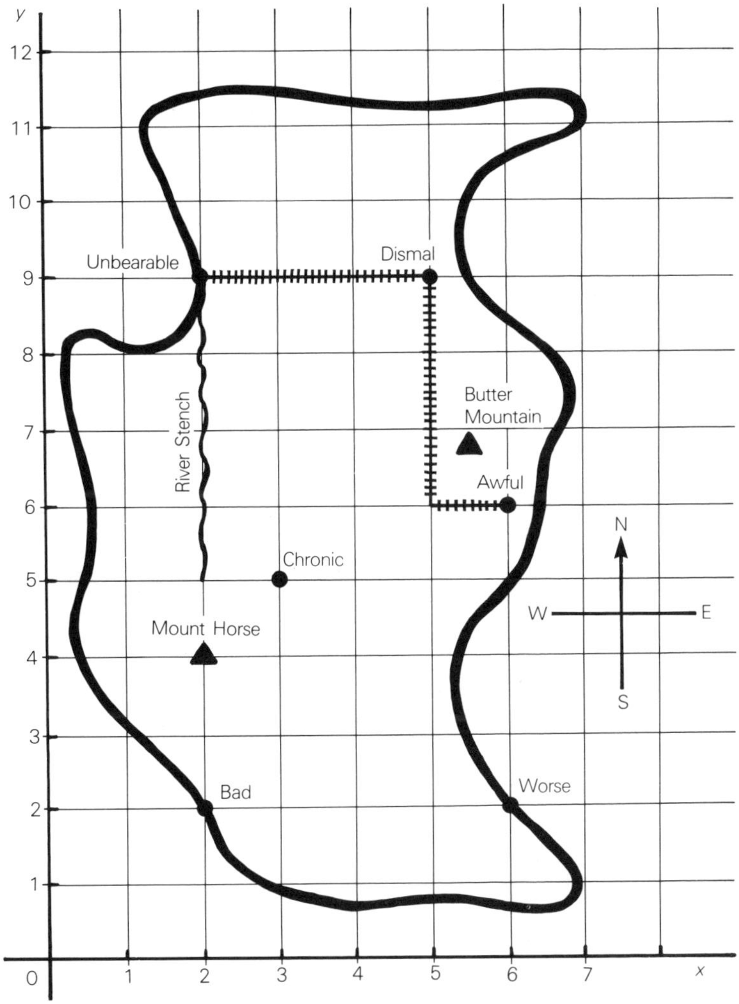

a) Write down the coordinates of Dismal.

b) Give the equation of the line the River Stench flows along.

c) Which towns lie on the line $y = x$?

d) There are plans to build a road going from Bad to Worse. What would be the equation of this road?

e) If you left Chronic and walked due east, what are the coordinates of the spot where you would reach the sea?

f) There is a railway line from Unbearable to Awful. What are the equations of the 3 lines it goes along?

g) Appalling New Town is to be built exactly half-way between Chronic and Dismal. What are its coordinates?

2

Draw axes with x and y going from 0 to 15 in each direction.

Draw these lines on your graph. Use 3, 6, 9 as your inputs.

a) $y = \frac{x}{3}$ b) $y = x - 2$ c) $y = 2x - 5$

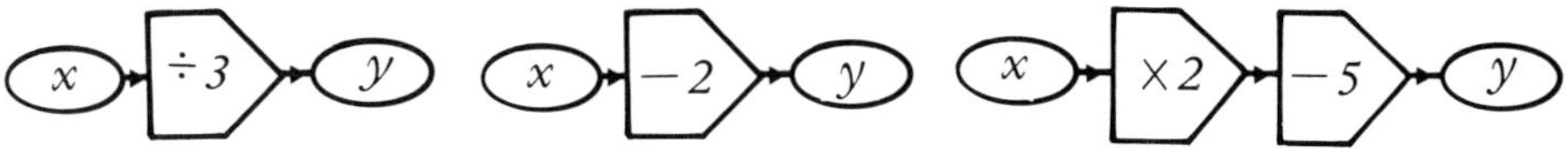

3

Copy the diagrams below and complete the equations.

a) 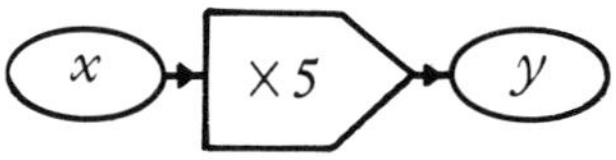

$y = \ldots$

b) 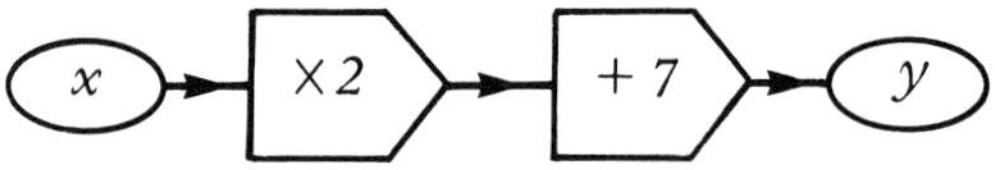

$y = \ldots$

c) 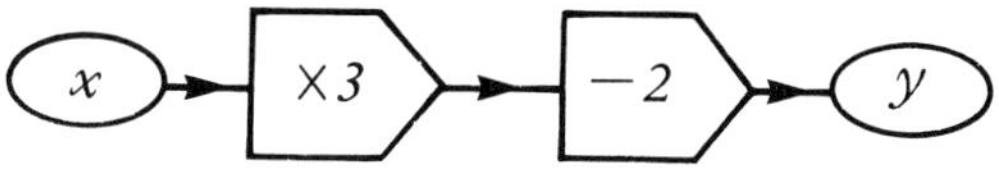

$y = \ldots$

4

Work out what these number machines must be. Show your answer by drawing the machine with its details inside the box. For example your answer might be 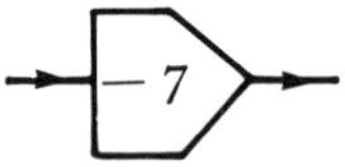

a)

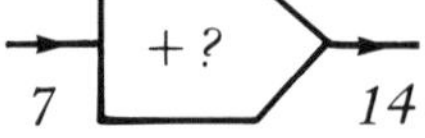

b)

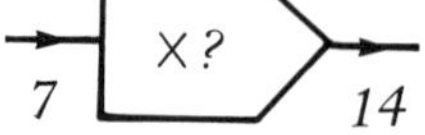

c)

d)

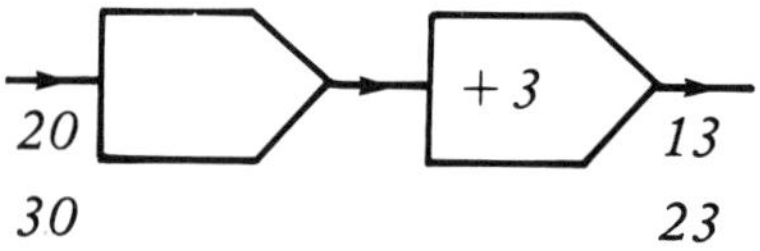

e)

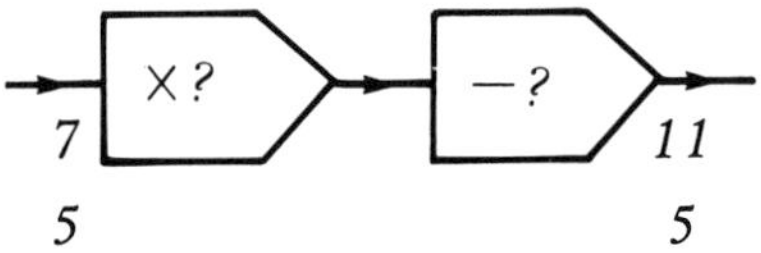

1

While tidying up his attic, Professor Mildew discovered a box of old number machines. Some of them looked broken, and most of them had lost their labels, but he thought he would try a few experiments anyway.

a) "This one looks in good condition – no label though. Let's see what happens." The Professor took a handful of numbers out of his pocket and put a 6 in. An 18 came out. "Hmmm. It must be a ×*3* " he muttered.

"Don't be such an ass, Mildew," cried his wife, who had overheard this. "It's a + *12* – plain as a pikestaff!"

To check, Professor Mildew put another number in, and a 24 came out. "What did I tell you"? said his wife. And the Professor had to admit she was right.

What was the second number the Professor put in?

b) The second machine was in a bad state. The digital mangle was bent, and mice were nesting in the numerical analyser. When he had straightened things out a little the Professor tried a few numbers:

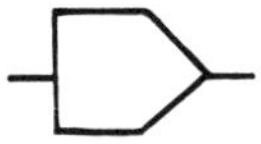

12 ⟶ 6
5 ⟶ 5
9 ⟶ 3
18 ⟶ 9
15 ⟶ 5
11 ⟶ 11
49 ⟶ 7
22 ⟶ 11

The machine certainly wasn't working properly, but after a little thought the Professor realised what it was doing. Can you work it out? What would come out if he put these numbers in next?

20 ⟶ ?
25 ⟶ ?
33 ⟶ ?
999 ⟶ ?

2

The next box of machines came from certain experiments Professor Mildew had carried out when he was a young man. He had taken an ordinary 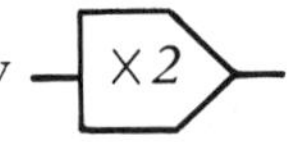

machine and bent the "out" tube round so that it sent the number coming out right back into the machine:

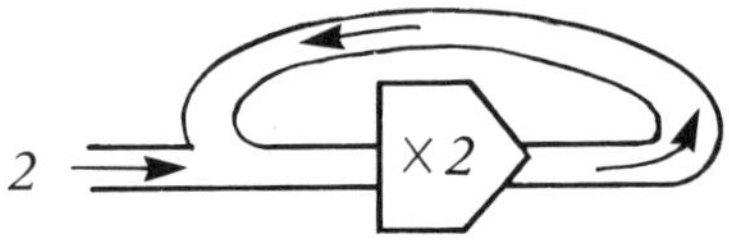

So if you put a 2 in to start with, a 4 would come out and be sent through the machine again, producing an 8, then a 16, then a 32, then a 64 . . .

The trouble was that machines like these got very overheated, and some had exploded, badly damaging several important numbers (and several important mathematicians). The Government banned them unless they were fitted with a safety valve. The valve worked like this: as soon as any number greater than 100 was produced it would come out through the valve and the machine would stop automatically.

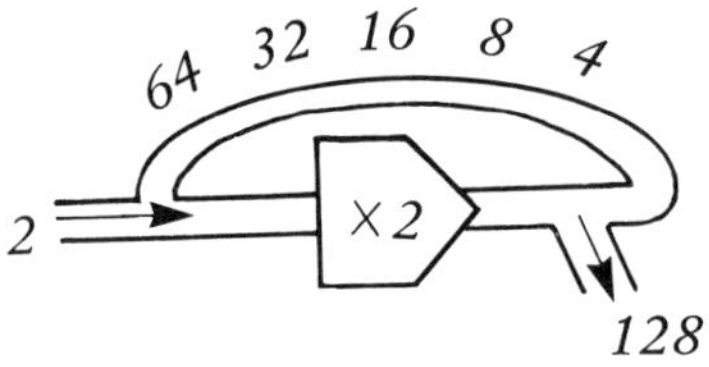

In the case shown here, the numbers that go through are *2*, *4*, *8*, *16*, *32*, *64*, *128*. The first number greater than *100* is *128*, so it comes out and the machine stops.

What numbers would come out of the safety valve in these cases?

a)

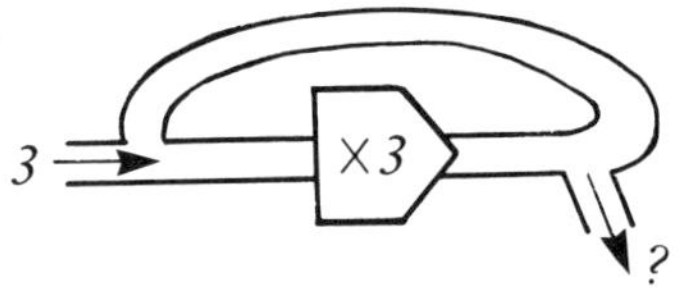

b)

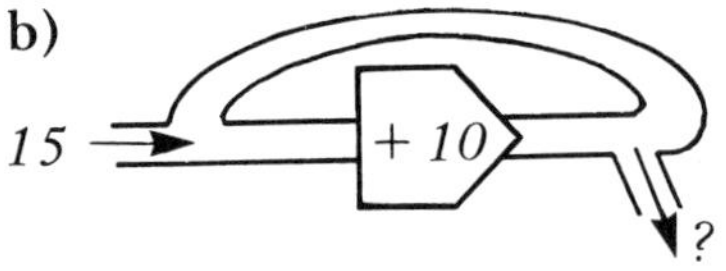

c)

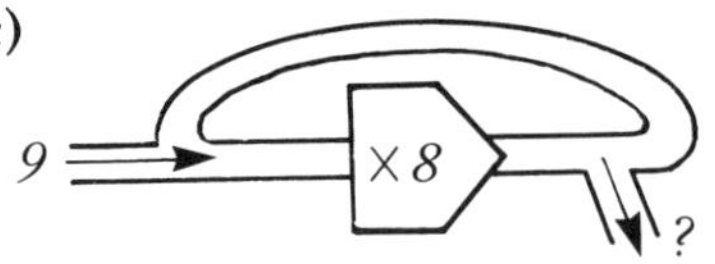

d)

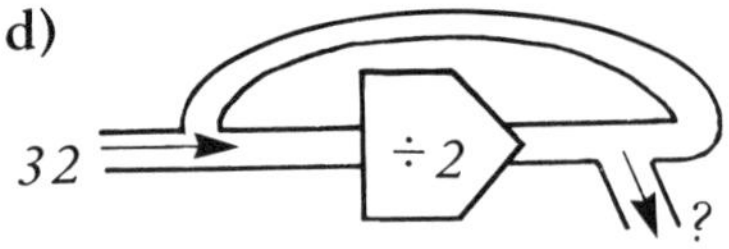

e)

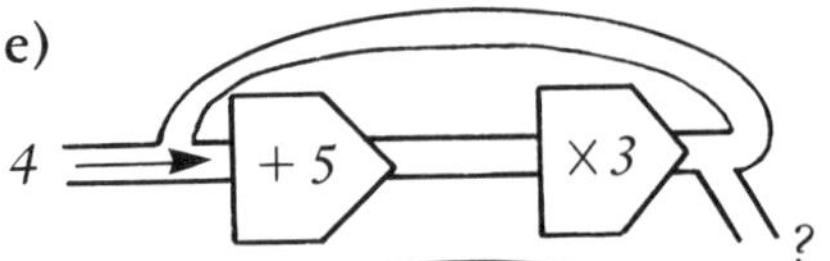

f)

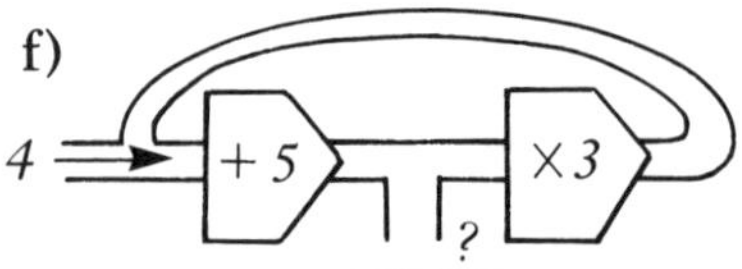

g)

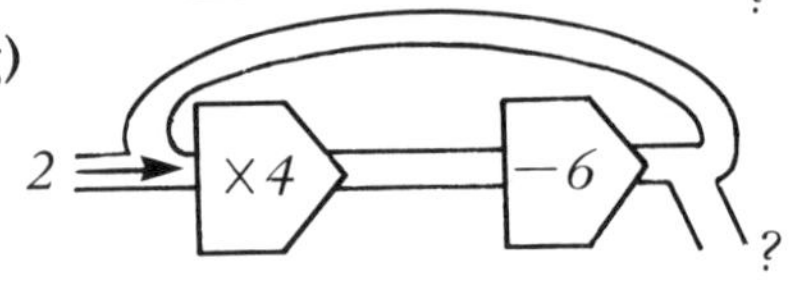

h)

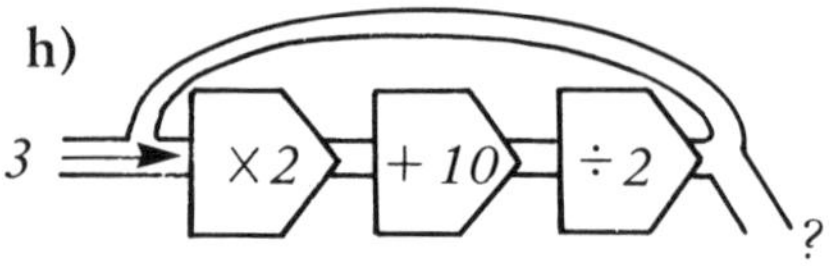

i) What was the number that was put in? It was a whole number, and it was less than 10.

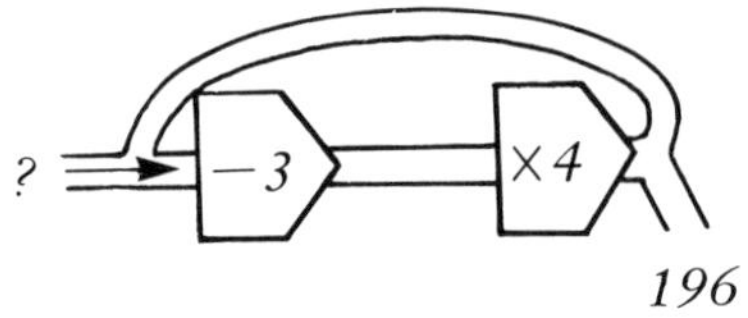

10. FRACTIONS III

PRACTICE 1 (ABC)

Remember:

$$\frac{3}{4} \div 6 = \frac{3}{4} \div \frac{6}{1} = \frac{1}{6} \text{ of } \frac{3}{4} = \frac{1}{6} \times \frac{3}{4} = \frac{3}{4} \times \frac{1}{6}$$

1

Work these out:

a) $6 \times \frac{3}{4}$ b) $8 \times \frac{5}{6}$ c) $12 \times \frac{3}{8}$ d) $7 \times \frac{2}{5}$

e) $9 \times \frac{2}{3}$ f) $20 \times \frac{1}{6}$

2

Work these out:

a) $\frac{3}{5} \times \frac{1}{2}$ b) $\frac{5}{7} \times \frac{2}{3}$ c) $\frac{2}{3} \times \frac{9}{10}$ d) $\frac{3}{4} \times \frac{4}{5}$

e) $\frac{1}{2} \times \frac{5}{9}$ f) $\frac{5}{8} \times \frac{6}{7}$

3

Work out:

a) $(12 + 8) \div 4$ b) $12 + (8 \div 4)$ c) $(24 - 5) \times 4$

d) $(24 \div 6) + 2$ e) $24 \div (6 + 2)$ f) $(3 \times 4) \times 5$

g) $3 \times (4 \times 5)$ h) $(12 + 15) \div (6 \div 2)$

4

Do these multiplications, simplifying first when possible:

a) $\frac{5}{9} \times \frac{6}{7}$ b) $\frac{15}{16} \times \frac{7}{10}$ c) $\frac{3}{5} \times \frac{10}{11}$ d) $\frac{2}{3} \times \frac{4}{9}$

5

a) In your book mark off a large square which is 6 little squares in each direction.

Put a ○ inside $\frac{2}{3}$ of the squares. Now put a X inside $\frac{3}{4}$ of the squares that have a ○ inside.

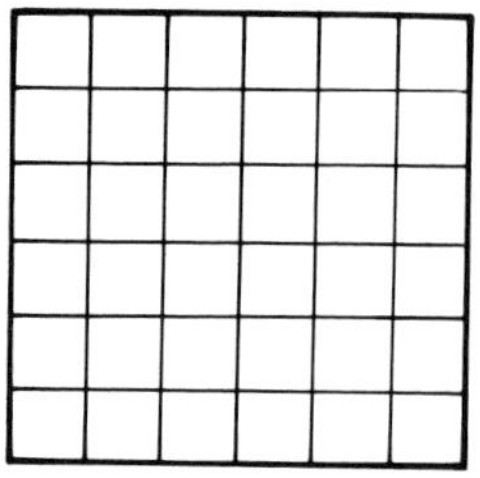

What fraction of all the squares have a ⊗ inside?

b) Work out: $\frac{2}{3} \times \frac{3}{4}$

6

Put in signs *and* brackets to make these work:

Question:	12 6 3 = 5
Answer:	$(12 \div 6) + 3 = 5$

a) 6 8 2 = 7 b) 3 2 1 = 7

c) 4 2 3 = 5 d) 4 2 3 = 6

e) 12 2 2 = 3 f) 2 8 5 = 6

7

Do these multiplications. There is an example in the box to remind you how to do them.

$$3\tfrac{1}{3} \times 1\tfrac{2}{5}$$
$$= \frac{\overset{2}{\cancel{10}}}{3} \times \frac{7}{\underset{1}{\cancel{5}}}$$
$$= \frac{14}{3}$$
$$= 4\tfrac{2}{3}$$

a) $1\frac{4}{5} \times 1\frac{1}{3}$ b) $3\frac{2}{3} \times 2\frac{2}{5}$ c) $3\frac{1}{5} \times \frac{3}{4}$ d) $2\frac{1}{4} \times 2\frac{2}{3}$

8

Do this multiplication. You can simplify any number on the top with any number on the bottom.

$$\frac{1}{2}\times\frac{2}{3}\times\frac{3}{4}\times\frac{4}{5}\times\frac{5}{6}\times\frac{6}{7}\times\frac{7}{8}$$

PRACTICE 2 (DE)

1

Work these out:

a) $12\div\frac{3}{4}$ b) $8\div\frac{2}{3}$ c) $10\div\frac{3}{4}$ d) $5\div\frac{1}{3}$

e) $6\div\frac{4}{5}$ f) $2\div\frac{4}{3}$

2

Look at the example in the box to remind you how to do these divisions.

$\frac{3}{10}\div\frac{2}{5}$

$=\frac{3}{\cancel{10}_{2}}\times\frac{\cancel{5}^{1}}{2}$

$=\frac{3}{4}$

a) $\frac{3}{4}\div\frac{2}{5}$ b) $\frac{7}{8}\div\frac{3}{4}$ c) $\frac{2}{5}\div\frac{2}{3}$ d) $\frac{5}{6}\div\frac{3}{8}$

e) $\frac{2}{7}\div\frac{4}{5}$ f) $\frac{4}{11}\div\frac{8}{11}$

3

Work these out:

a) $\frac{7}{9}\div\frac{5}{6}$ b) $\frac{3}{10}\div\frac{2}{15}$ c) $\frac{3}{8}\div\frac{1}{4}$ d) $\frac{11}{12}\div\frac{3}{8}$

4

Do these divisions of mixed numbers. There is an example in the box to help you.

$$\begin{aligned} & 4\tfrac{1}{2} \div 1\tfrac{1}{5} \\ &= \tfrac{9}{2} \div \tfrac{6}{5} \\ &= \tfrac{\cancel{9}^{3}}{2} \times \tfrac{5}{\cancel{6}_{2}} \\ &= \tfrac{15}{4} \\ &= 3\tfrac{3}{4} \end{aligned}$$

a) $3\frac{3}{4} \div 1\frac{2}{3}$ b) $2\frac{1}{2} \div 1\frac{1}{2}$ c) $2\frac{1}{10} \div \frac{7}{8}$ d) $1\frac{1}{4} \div 1\frac{5}{6}$

5

a) A bar of soap lasts Egbert 30 days. How many bars of soap will he use in 120 days?

b) A bar of chocolate lasts Egbert $1\frac{1}{4}$ minutes. How many bars of chocolate will he eat in 120 minutes? (Given the opportunity, that is.)

6

a) $5\frac{1}{4} + 2\frac{1}{3}$ b) $5\frac{1}{4} - 2\frac{1}{3}$ c) $5\frac{1}{4} \times 2\frac{1}{3}$ d) $5\frac{1}{4} \div 2\frac{1}{3}$

7

There are 30 pies at a party. If each person gets $\frac{2}{3}$ of a pie, how many people can be given some? The answer to $30 \div \frac{2}{3}$ tells you.

a) Work out: $30 \div \frac{2}{3}$

Now work out how many people can be given some if each person is given:

b) $\frac{3}{4}$ of a pie   c) $\frac{2}{5}$ of a pie   d) $\frac{5}{8}$ of a pie   e) $\frac{5}{6}$ of a pie

SUMMARY

1

Do these 10 short questions:

a) $(12+13)\times(14+15)$

b) $15\overline{)3135}$

c) How many 18 p stamps could you buy for £4.50?

d) Put in brackets to make this work: $\frac{1}{2}+\frac{1}{3}\times\frac{1}{4} = \frac{5}{24}$

e) Carol divided 91980 by 7, and then divided the answer by 5. Lucy divided 91980 by 6, and then divided the answer by 6. Which of the two girls ended up with the larger final answer?

f) $(3\frac{3}{4}-1\frac{1}{2})\times 2\frac{2}{5}$

g) Depending how you put in the brackets, you can get two different answers to this division:

$$120 \div 12 \div 2$$

What are the possible answers?

h) $(11+?)\div(?-1)=4$.
The question mark stands for the same number in both places. What does it stand for?

i) $1\frac{1}{2}\times 1\frac{1}{2}\times 1\frac{1}{2}$

j) Find the area of the rectangle:

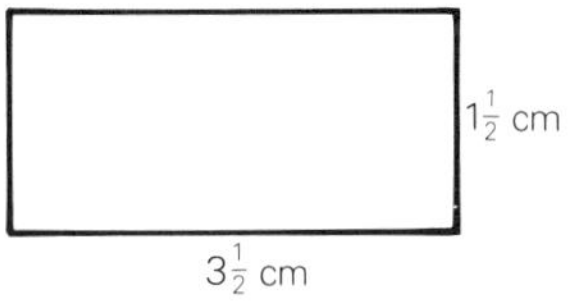

2

Work out:

a) $\frac{3}{4}+\frac{2}{3}$ b) $\frac{3}{4}-\frac{2}{3}$ c) $\frac{3}{4}\times\frac{2}{3}$ d) $\frac{3}{4}\div\frac{2}{3}$

3

a) (A very easy question.) Lord Connick-Section, the owner of Hyperbola Hall, always walks at a speed of 5 km/h. How far would he walk in 2 hours?

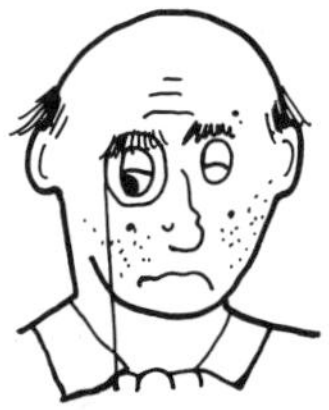

b) (A harder question – think how you did (a) to help you.) Slobber, Lord Connick-Section's rather ancient butler, always walks at $3\frac{1}{3}$ km/h. How far would he walk in $\frac{3}{4}$ of an hour?

4

a) $2\frac{1}{3} - 1\frac{5}{6} + 3\frac{4}{9}$ b) $8 \times 1\frac{2}{3}$ c) $4 - 1\frac{5}{6}$ d) $(\frac{1}{3} \div \frac{1}{2}) + \frac{1}{4}$

5

a) A lesson lasts $\frac{3}{4}$ hour. How many lessons could be fitted in a 9-hour day, if there were no gaps between lessons?

b) At a scout camp each boy gets $\frac{2}{3}$ of a bun for breakfast.
   (i) How many buns will 18 boys eat altogether?
   (ii) How many boys would 18 buns feed?

6

a) There are 20 children in Form IIIa, and $\frac{3}{4}$ of them are girls. There are 18 children in Form IIIb, and $\frac{1}{3}$ of them are girls. How many girls are there in both forms put together?

b) Work out: $\left(\frac{3}{5} \text{ of } £1.20\right) - \left(\frac{1}{6} \text{ of } £2.70\right)$

ALLSORTS

1

At a certain school $\frac{3}{4}$ of the children are stupid. $\frac{2}{5}$ of the stupid children are also ugly. $\frac{5}{6}$ of the stupid ugly children are ill-mannered.

What fraction of the children are stupid, ugly and ill-mannered?

2

At a party the 12 girls were each given $\frac{3}{4}$ of a cake, and the boys were each given $\frac{2}{3}$ of a cake. Altogether 15 cakes were eaten. How many boys were there?

3

Sometimes we need more than one lot of brackets in an expression. The rule is: work out anything in ordinary brackets () first; then do the curly brackets{ }; finally do the square brackets[] .

Work out the value of this expression:

$$999 \div [3 \times \{72 \div (52-44)\}]$$

4

By putting in signs and brackets we can make many numbers from just four 2s. There is an example in the box opposite.

Question:	2 2 2 2 = 4
Answer:	(2 × 2)+2 − 2 = 4

Do these in the same way:

a) 2 2 2 2 = 12

b) 2 2 2 2 = 2

c) 2 2 2 2 = 6

d) 2 2 2 2 = 1.5

5

On the right is a fairly typical sample of Shelley's exercise book. He had just done a multiplication of fractions (correctly, as it happens). Then he started to change his cartridge, "and it suddenly exploded, just by itself", he explained to Mr Abel afterwards. He couldn't explain the fingerprints, "but somebody else must have done them while I was looking for my blotting-paper."

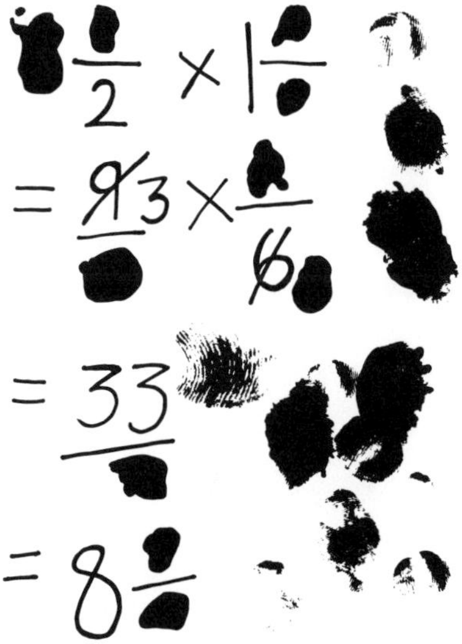

Can you write out the sum clearly? (Each small blot just hides one number.)

6

a) For fanatics of division of fractions:

$$14\tfrac{1}{16} \div 5\tfrac{25}{28}$$

b) For long division fanatics:

$$19\overline{)999\,999\,999\,999\,999\,999}$$

(There are 18 nines altogether.)

7

Some rather unusual bathroom tiles are this shape:

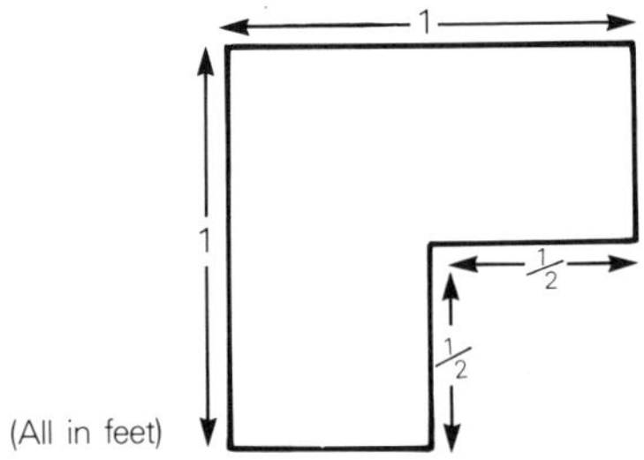

How many of these tiles would be needed to cover a rectangle which is 6 feet long and 4 feet high?

8

Of course Milly has to do her brackets the wrong way round. So for instance)2 + 3(× 4 means "work out 2 + 3, then multiply the answer by 4" – giving the answer 20. Work out the Milly-value of:

$$\frac{)109 + 19(\div)76 \div 19(}{)3 + 1(\times 4}$$

11. PRIMES AND INDICES

PRACTICE 1 (AB)

1

Write these out, putting the correct number in place of the question mark:

a) $2^8 \times 2^4 = 2^?$ b) $5^3 \times 5^4 = 5^?$

c) $3^6 \times 3^2 = 3^?$ d) $10^6 \times 10^6 = 10^?$

e) $n^4 \times n^7 = n^?$ f) $a^2 \times a^3 = a^?$

g) $2^? \times 2^3 = 2^9$ h) $4^2 \times 4^2 \times 4^2 = 4^?$

i) $y^4 \times y^? = y^{20}$ j) $3^4 \times 3^? = 3^7 \times 3^6$

2

Work out the value of these. Don't try to do too much in your head.

a) 2^6 b) 9^2 c) 6^3 d) 1^7 e) 17^2 f) 20^2

g) $\frac{1}{2}^2$ h) 3^5

3

When Mr Abel has marked a maths exam he never puts the results up in a straightforward way. Here is one of his lists:

Form V	Maths Exam
	(%)
Angus	$2 \times 5 \times 7$
Ben	2×29
Emma	$2^4 \times 5$
Fatima	$2^2 \times 3^2$
Fiona	7×11
Hamish	$3^2 \times 7$
Oliver	$2^2 \times 11$
Tom	3^4

As you can see, the children have been listed in alphabetical order and the marks have been put as the product of prime factors. It's not even clear who came top.

Work out each child's mark and write out the list in order, starting with the top mark.

4

Mr Delta's geography results are shown on the right.

Rewrite the geography list as Mr Abel would have put it: with the children alphabetically, and the marks written as the product of prime factors.

Geography Exam	(%)
Fiona	84
Ben	75
Fatima	60
Tom	54
Emma	50
Hamish	48
Angus	30
Oliver	27

PRACTICE 2 (CDE)

1

Write these numbers as the product of prime factors:

a) 108 b) 100 c) 76 d) 126

2

Find:

a) the HCF of 36 and 90

b) the HCF of 28 and 210

c) the LCM of 12 and 16

d) the LCM of 21 and 35

e) $\sqrt{196}$

f) $\sqrt{324}$

3

Tom has been going around challenging people to answer this problem, and laughing in a superior way when they get it wrong;

"A square has area 225 cm^2. What is its perimeter?"

Fatima managed to remember that a square had 4 sides, but couldn't decide whether to multiply or divide by 4. Then Tom told her that both would be wrong.

By writing 225 as the product of prime factors, find how long each side of the square is, and so find the perimeter.

4

As a punishment for eating chocolate éclairs in class, Egbert has been set a rather nasty addition of fractions to do:

$$\frac{7}{30}+\frac{5}{42} = \frac{?}{?}+\frac{?}{?} = \frac{?}{?}$$

The trouble is that he can't even find a number that 30 and 42 will both divide into.

Of course what he wants is the LCM of 30 and 42. Find it, and finish the sum.

5

Write these out, putting the correct number in place of the question mark:

a) $2^{12} \div 2^4 = 2^?$ b) $4^8 \div 4^5 = 4^?$ c) $c^5 \div c^4 = c^?$

d) $m^{15} \div m^7 = m^?$ e) $2^? \div 2^3 = 2^3$ f) $a^4 \times a^5 \div a^7 = a^?$

6

Find the HCF of 198 and 330.

7

Calculate the value of the following. If you remember the rules for multiplying and dividing numbers with indices, *there is no difficult multiplying or dividing to do*:

Example: $2^{11} \div 2^9 = 2^2 = 4$

a) $3^6 \div 3^4$ b) $2^3 \times 2^4 \div 2^6$ c) $\sqrt{5^4}$ d) $9^9 \div 9^7$

8

Write 999 as the product of prime factors.

SUMMARY

1

Answer these 10 short questions:

a) $2^{10} = 1024$. Work out the value of 2^{11}.

b) Write 180 as the product of prime factors.

c) Find the value of 11^3.

d) Find the square root of 256.

e) $2^5 + 2^5 = 2^?$. What does the question mark stand for? (Not 10!)

f) Find the LCM of 12 and 21.

g) Find the value of $2 \times 5^2 \times 7$.

h) Write out the following, putting the correct number in place of the question mark:

$$e^5 \times e^2 \times e = e^?$$

i) $3^8 = 6561$. Use this to find 3^7.

j) Remembering what you were told in (i), find $\sqrt{6561}$.

2

Here is a table of powers of 2:

2^1	= 2	2^6	= 64
2^2	= 4	2^7	= 128
2^3	= 8	2^8	= 256
2^4	= 16	2^9	= 512
2^5	= 32	2^{10}	= 1024

Using this table, plus what we know about multiplying and dividing numbers with indices, we can do quite difficult sums very easily.

For example: what is 16×32?

$$\begin{aligned} &16 \times 32 \\ &= 2^4 \times 2^5 \\ &= 2^9 \\ &= 512 \end{aligned}$$

Some more examples:

$$1024 \div 64 = 2^{10} \div 2^6 = 2^4 = 16$$

$$16 \times 256 \div 64 = 2^4 \times 2^8 \div 2^6 = 2^6 = 64$$

Now do these, setting them out in the same way:

a) 32×32 b) 8×64 c) $512 \div 64$

d) $8 \times 8 \times 8$ e) $16 \times 128 \div 8$ f) $1024 \div 8$

3

a) Write as the product of prime factors: (i) 441, (ii) 90, (iii) 126.

b) Use your answers to (a) to find:
   (i) $\sqrt{441}$
   (ii) the HCF of 441 and 126
   (iii) the LCM of 126 and 90.

ALLSORTS

1

Mrs Haddock, the school cook, is famous for her baked beans. But her salads are also very popular.

If she is very busy, the salad is only ham and lettuce. You are allowed to choose just what you want, or even to have nothing at all. So there are 4 possibilities:

nothing
or H (which means just ham)
or L (which means just lettuce)
or H, L (which means ham and lettuce)

a) Sometimes the salad consists of ham, lettuce and tomato. Make a list of all the possibilities. How many are there altogether?

b) Make a list of all the possibilities if the salad is ham, lettuce, tomato and egg. How many are there altogether?

c) If the salad consisted of ham, lettuce, tomato, egg, coleslaw, potato, beetroot and onion, how many possibilities would there be? *Don't* try to make a list of them all.

2

a) Copy and complete this table:

$$11^2 = 121$$
$$12^2 = 144$$
$$13^2 = 169$$
$$\vdots$$
$$20^2 = 400$$

b) Now use the table to copy and complete this table:

$$11^2 - 10^2 = 21$$
$$12^2 - 11^2 = 23$$
$$\vdots$$
$$20^2 - 19^2 = 39$$

c) By spotting the pattern, write down the values of:
(i) $81^2 - 80^2$ (ii) $206^2 - 205^2$

3

Find the square root of 7056.

4

A product of prime factors has been half-wiped off the board:

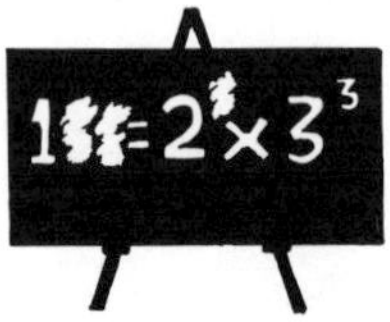

The squiggles stand for numbers that are impossible to read. Work out what it should say.

12. BEARINGS

PRACTICE 1 (AB)

1

The diagram below shows a school playing field. The dots show the exact spot where the places are, not the pictures.

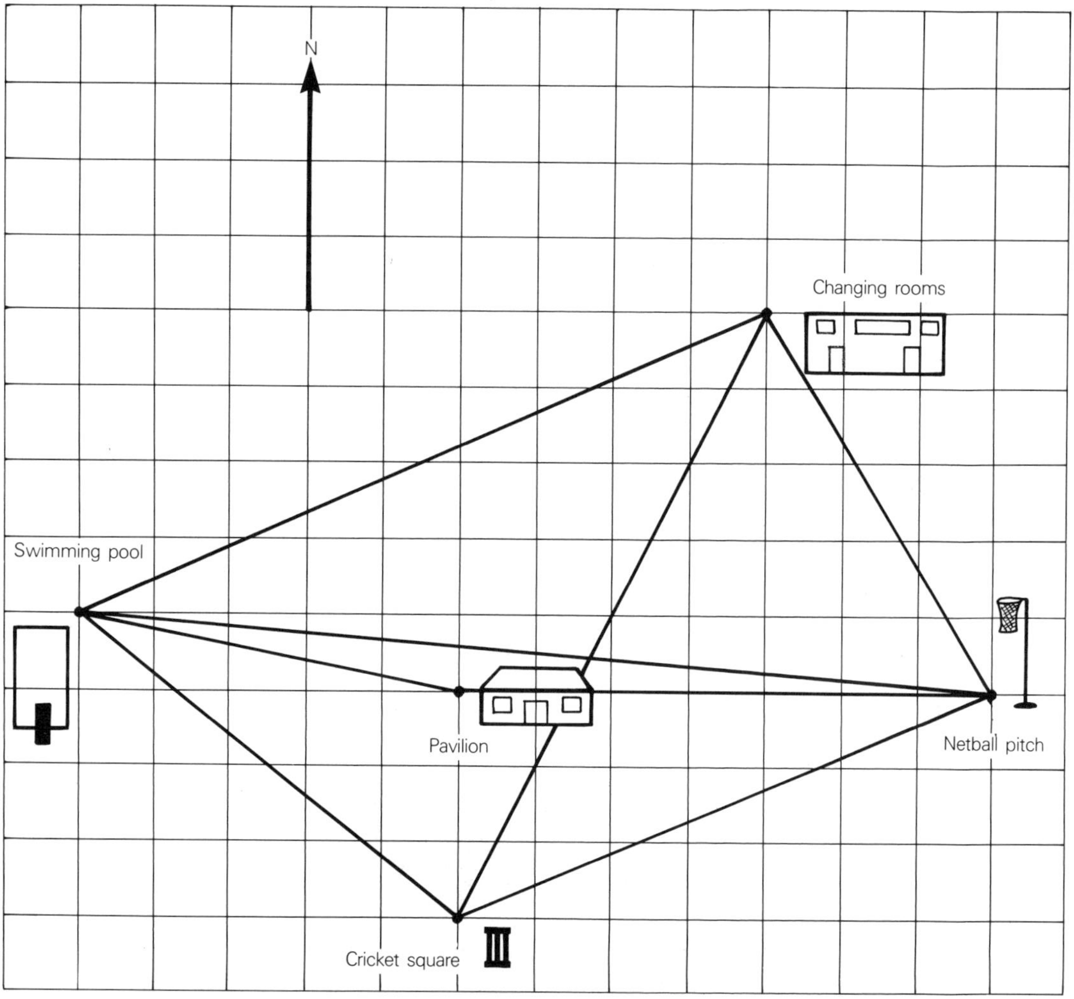

Find:

a) The bearing of the changing rooms from the swimming pool.

b) The bearing of the cricket square from the swimming pool.

c) The bearing of the changing rooms from the cricket square.

d) The bearing of the netball pitch from the pavilion.

e) The bearing of the cricket square from the pavilion.

f) The bearing of the netball pitch from the swimming pool.

g) The bearing of the netball pitch from the cricket square.

h) The bearing of the swimming pool from the changing rooms.

2

In each part of this question you have to find the bearings of B from A.

All the answers are greater than 180°.

The diagram on the right may help you to make sure your answers are sensible.

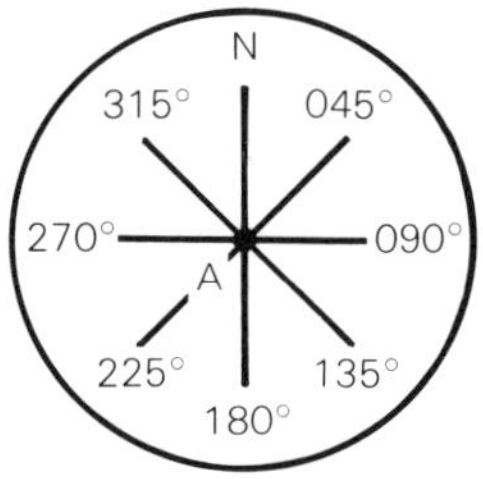

a)

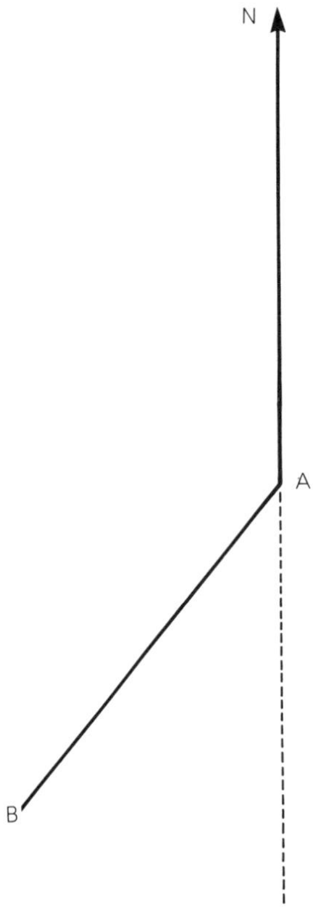

b)

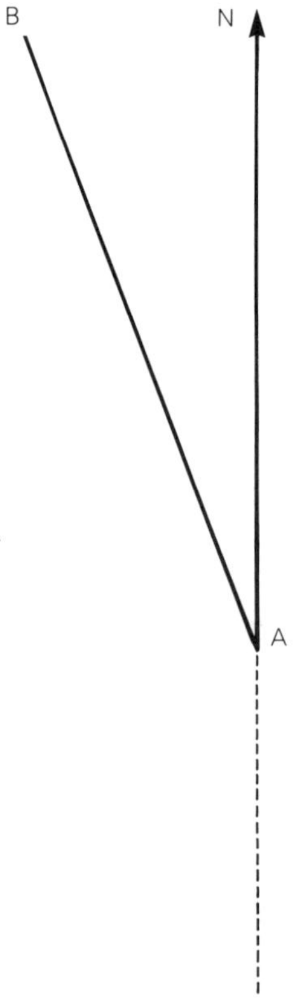

c)

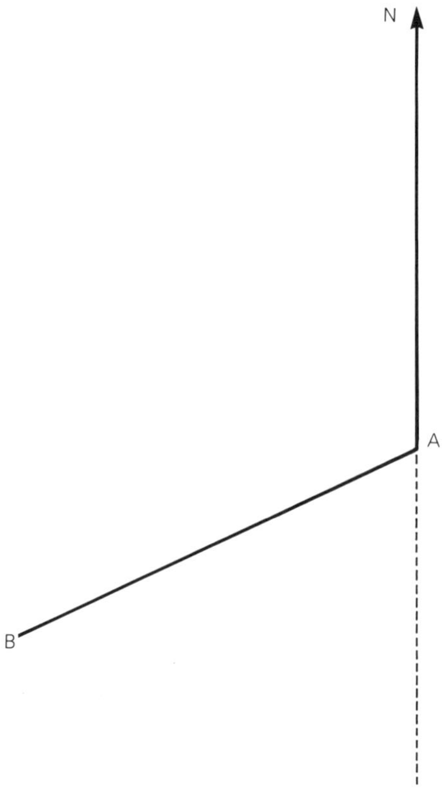

3

On the diagram below, measure the bearing of:

a) T from Q b) P from S c) R from T

d) R from P e) R from S f) S from Q

g) S from P.

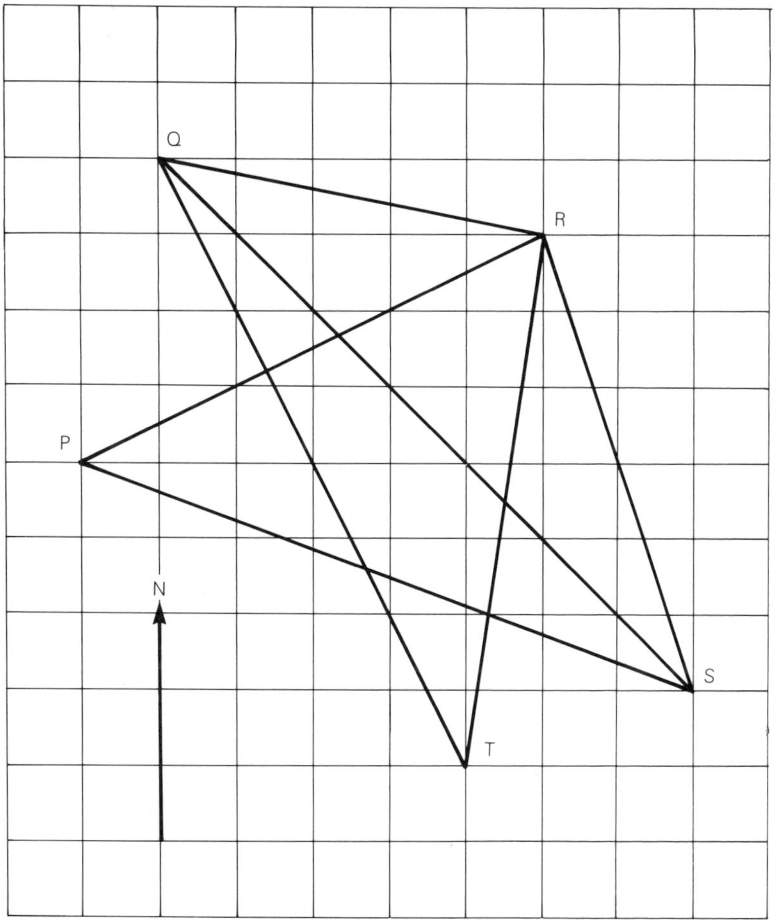

4

Take a new page for this question. Mark the point X with a small dot near the bottom left corner of the page.

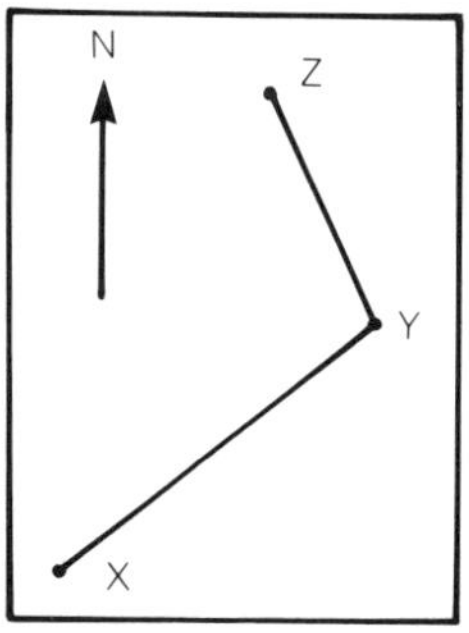

Y is 11 cm from X on a bearing of 052° from X.

Z is 7 cm from Y on a bearing of 335° from Y.

Taking north to be straight up the page, carefully mark Y and Z on your diagram.

Measure the bearing of X from Z.

PRACTICE 2 (CDEF)

1

Tom and Fatima are looking out of the windows at opposite ends of the school. The school buildings run from east to west, and the two windows are 80 m apart.

Mr Abel is standing in the middle of the field solving quadratic equations in his head. The bearing of Mr Abel from Tom is 066°, and the bearing of Mr Abel from Fatima is 035°.

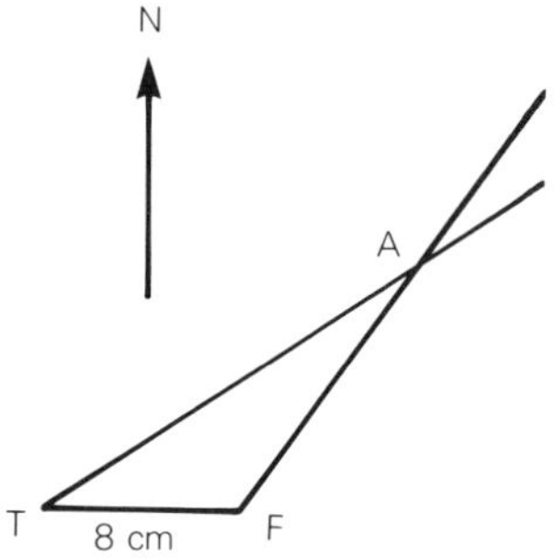

Using a scale of 1 cm to 10 m (so 80 m becomes 8 cm), make a scale drawing of the position of T, F and A.

How far is Mr Abel from Tom? (Answer in metres, not centimetres.)

2

a) The bearing of X from Y is 094°. What is the bearing of Y from X?

b) The bearing of D from E is 228°. What is the bearing of E from D?

c) The bearing of P from Q is 185°. What is the bearing of Q from P?

3

One Sunday a man takes a walk from A to B to C to D.

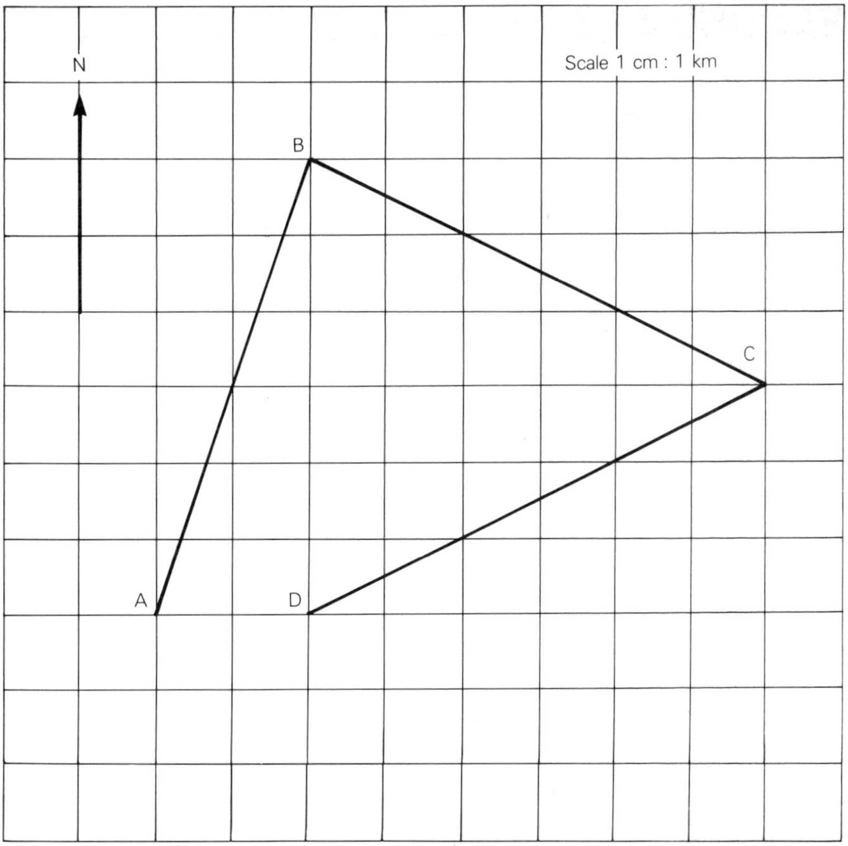

Copy out the following, putting the right numbers in place of the dots:

a) "To get from A to B walk . . . km on a bearing of . . . ° from A."

b) "To get from B to C walk . . . km on a bearing of . . . ° from B."

c) "To get from C to D walk . . . km on a bearing of . . . ° from C."

4

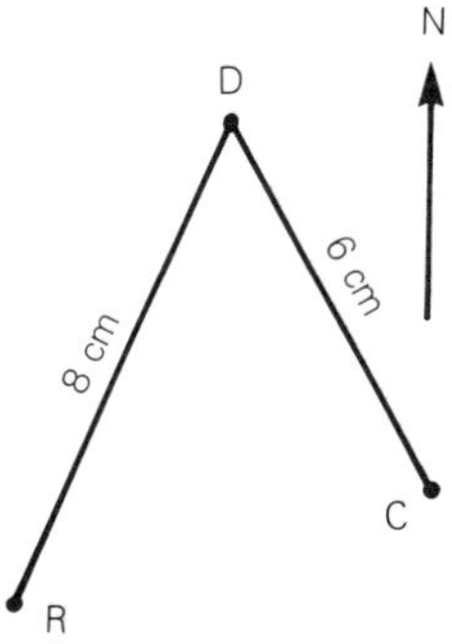

In the Admiral's study, a bottle of rum, R, is 8 m from the desk, D, on a bearing of 217° from D. The box of cigars, C, is 6 m from D on a bearing of 147° from D.

Make a scale drawing showing the positions of D, R and C. Use a scale of 1 cm to 1 m.

The Admiral has just taken a cigar from the box. Tell him exactly how he can get to the bottle of rum – how many metres he should walk, and on what bearing from C.

SUMMARY

1

Look at the diagram opposite, and make *sensible guesses* of the bearing of:

a) A from B b) C from D

c) D from A d) D from B

e) E from C f) A from E

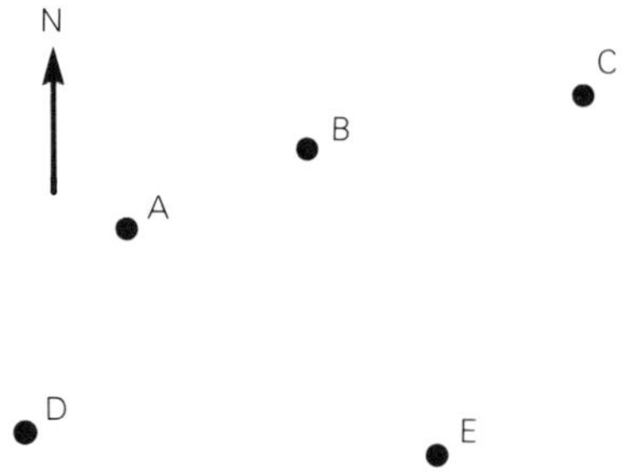

2

A river runs from east to west. A fox, F, is on the bank of the river, and 10 m west is a wolf, W, also on the bank of the river.

A chicken, C, lies sleeping peacefully on the opposite bank of the river. The bearing of C from W is 145° and the bearing of C from F is 230°.

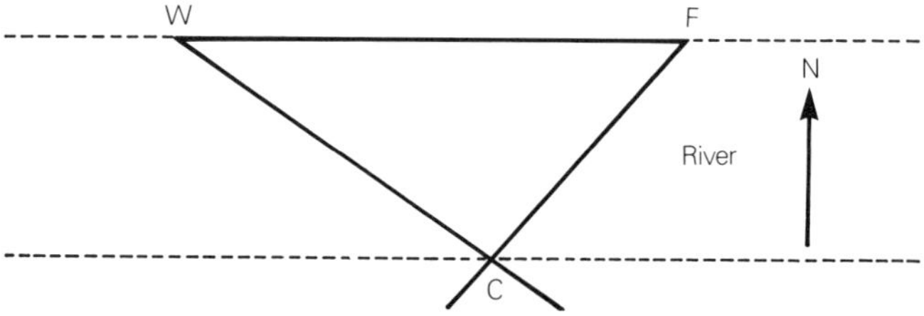

a) Using a scale of 1 cm to 1 m, make a scale drawing showing W, F and C.

b) How wide is the river? Answer in metres not centimetres.

c) The chicken sleepwalks 2 m due south of C. What are its new bearings from W and from F?

3

Mr and Mrs Deckchair want to travel from their home to Stenchmouth, where they always spend their summer holidays. Mr Deckchair has worked out the route he would like to take on the map on the next page, and so has Mrs Deckchair.

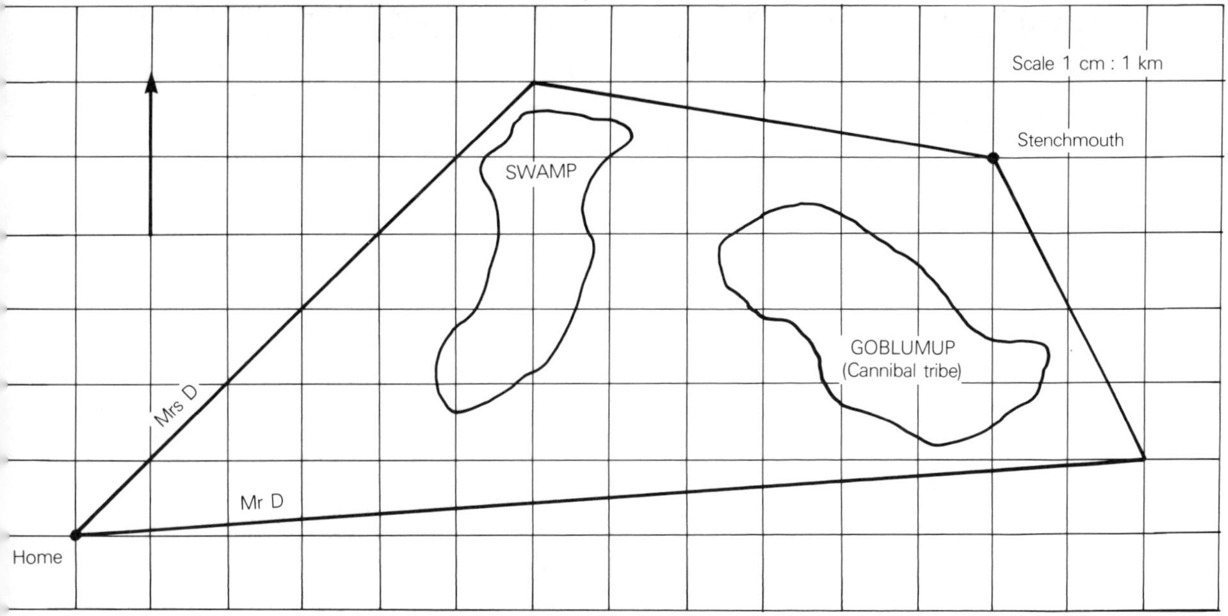

Describe the two routes carefully in the form "... km on a bearing of ..., then ... km on a bearing of ..."

ALLSORTS

1

a) John walks 1 km due north, then 1 km on a bearing of 090°, then 1 km on a bearing of 180°, then 1 km on a bearing of 270°.

   Make a rough sketch of his path.

b) Another day John walks 1 km due north, then 1 km on a bearing of 030°, then 1 km on a bearing of 060°, then 1 km on a bearing of 090°, then 1 km on a bearing of 120° and so on, finishing with 1 km on a bearing of 330°.

   Make a rough sketch of his path.

2

A lane runs due north. At a certain point in the lane, P, the bearing of the church (from P) is 055°. 20 m further north along the lane is a point Q, and the bearing of the church from Q is 070°.

Using a scale of 1 mm to 1 m, make a scale drawing showing P, Q and the church.

a) 10 m north of Q is R. What is the bearing of the church from R?

b) As you walk north along the road, how far are you from the church when you are nearest to it?

3

Draw an equilateral triangle with sides 6 cm long. Label it ABC as in the diagram opposite.

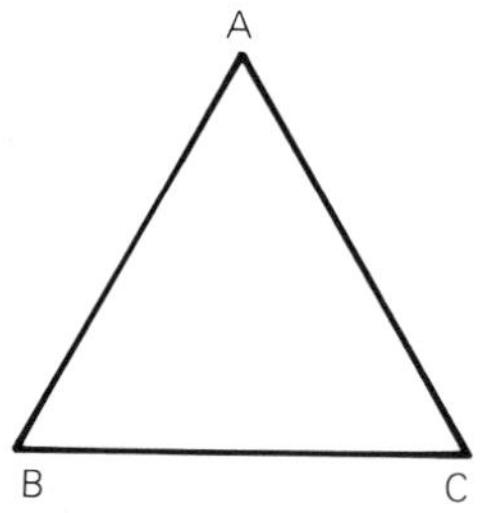

The bearing of B from C is 300°. Mark in a north line. What is the bearing of B from A?

4

The bearing of X from Y is 220°, and XY = 5 cm. The bearing of Z from Y is 110°. The bearing of Z from X is 080°.

Make a drawing showing X, Y and Z.

5

ABCDEF is a regular hexagon. If you know a little about regular hexagons you can do this question without any measuring – just by thinking.

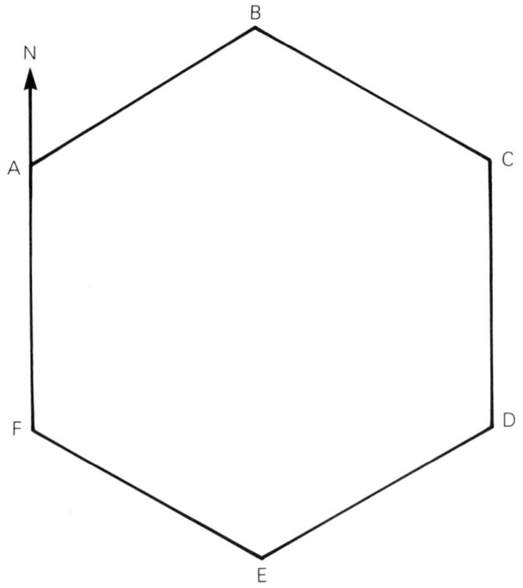

Find the bearing of:

a) B from A	b) D from E	c) E from B	d) A from C
e) D from A	f) F from C	g) B from C	h) B from F

13. MEASUREMENT II

PRACTICE 1 (A)

1

Find the area of these rectangles, remembering to give your answer in the correct units:

a) **b)** **c)** **d)**

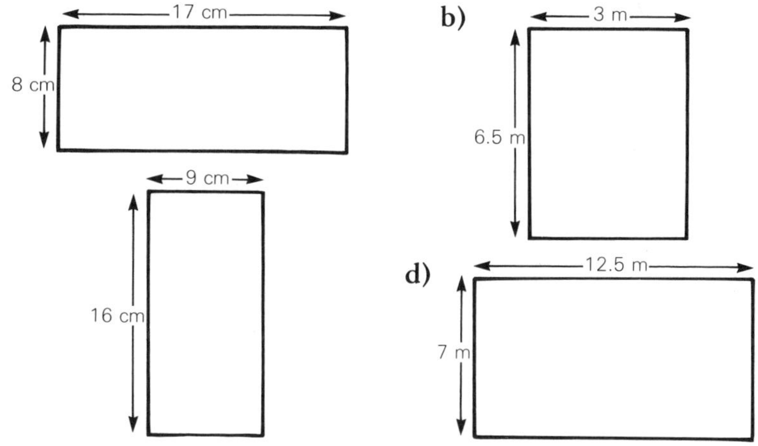

2

In the Republic of Mania, short lengths are measured in guz.

The diagram below shows a circle of radius 4 guz.

Find its area by counting squares.

(Each square is 1 guz long.)

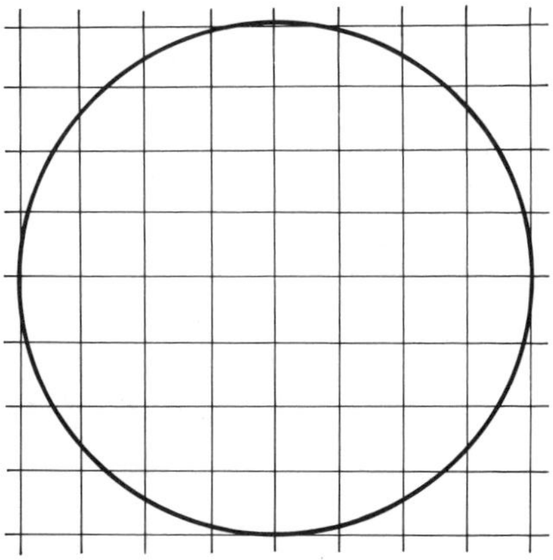

3

Find the area of these triangles:

a)

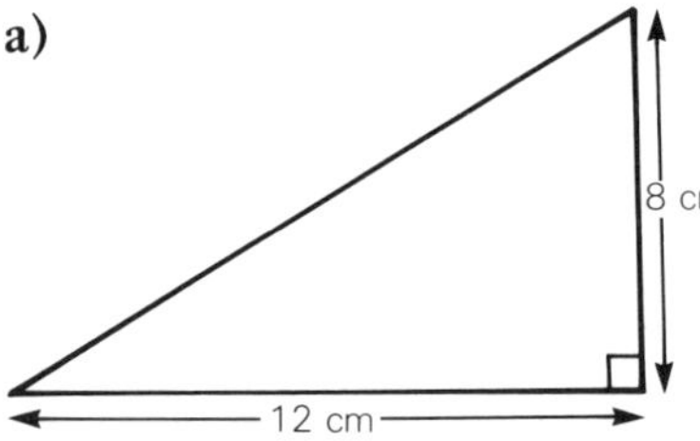

b)

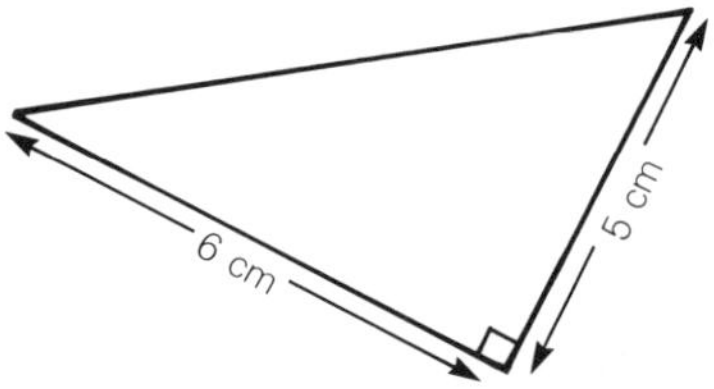

c)

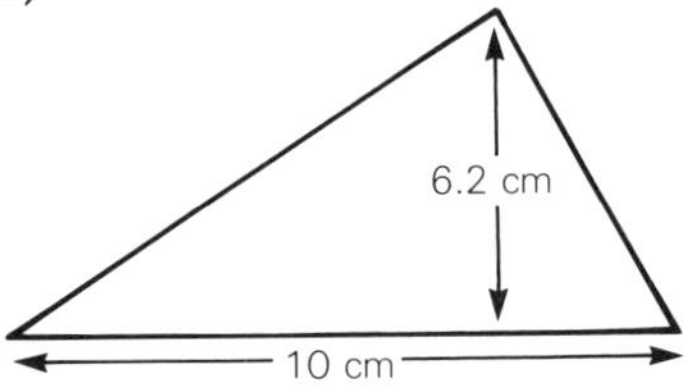

d)

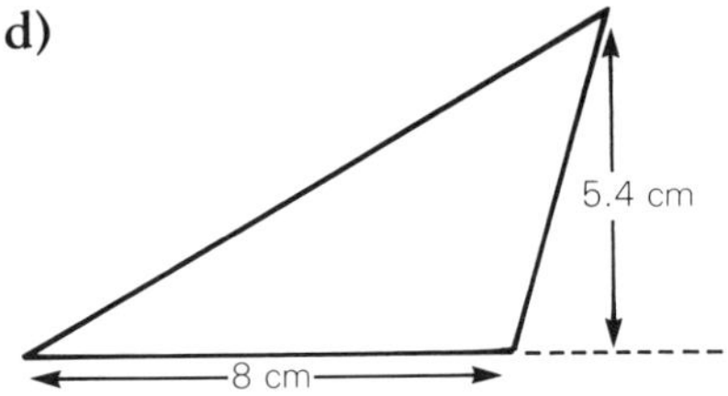

e)

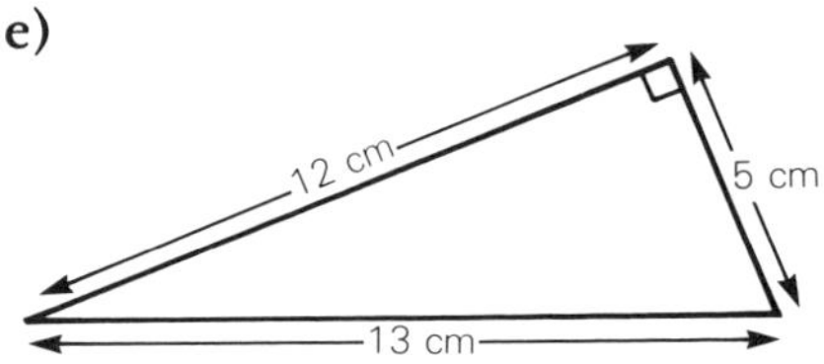

4

Find the area of these quadrilaterals:

a)

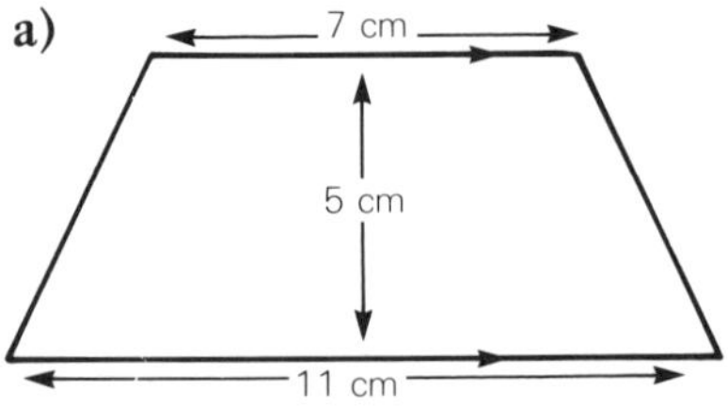

b)

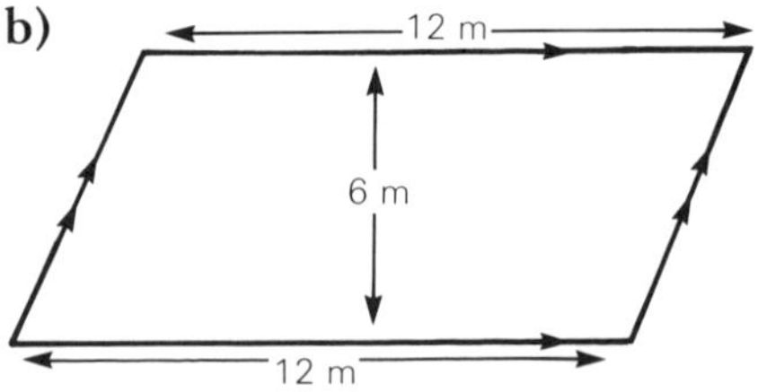

c)

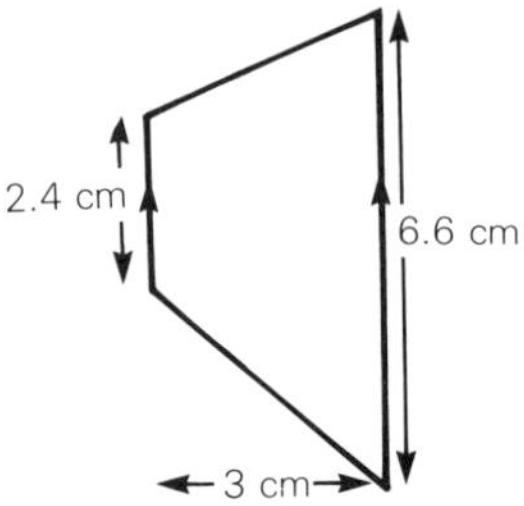

5

Find the dotted area (all measurements are in cm):

a)

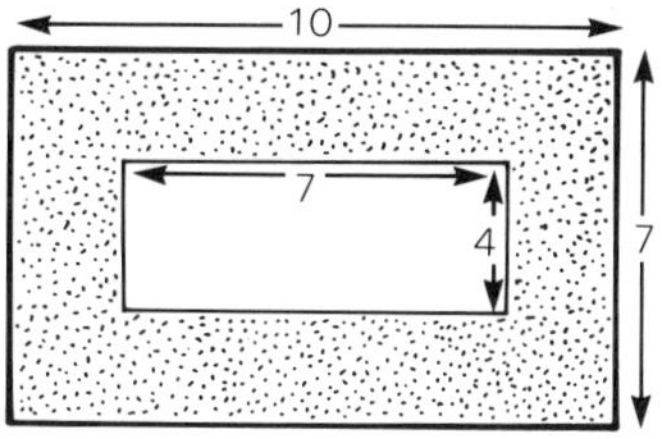

b)

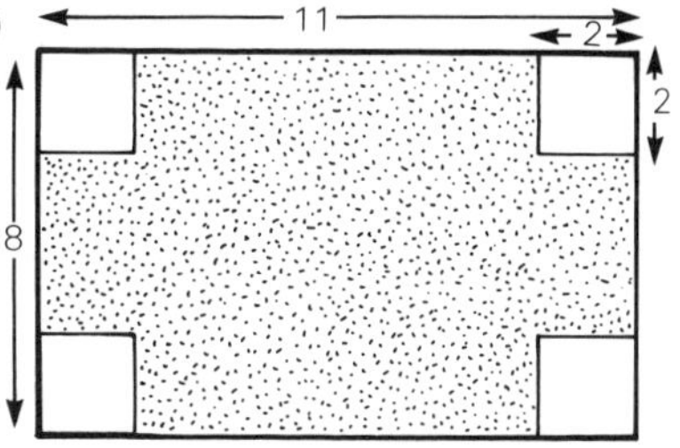

All 4 little squares are 2 cm by 2 cm

c)

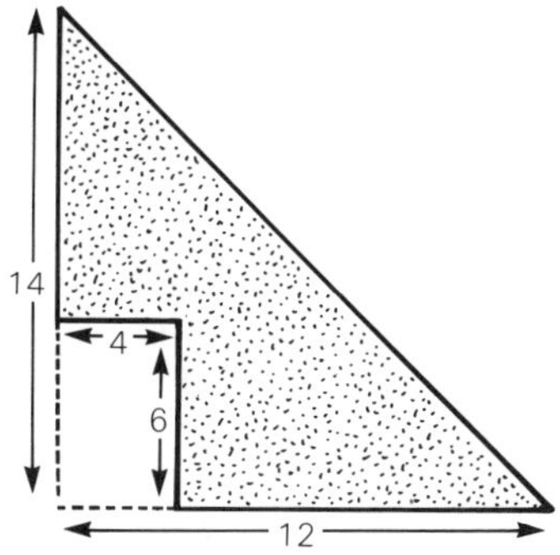

6

Each of the diagrams below can be divided into two rectangles by a dotted line. Copy each diagram. Work out the missing lengths shown with a question mark (all measurements are in cm), and write in your answers. Now you can find the area of each of the rectangles that make up the diagram; write these inside the rectangles. Finally, write underneath the *total* area of the diagram.

Here is an example:

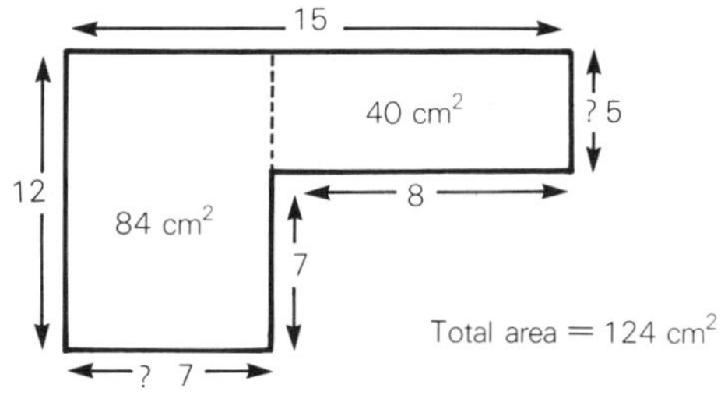

a)

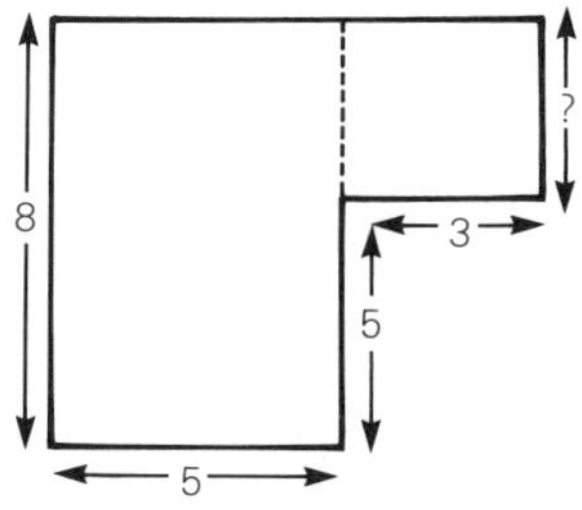

b)

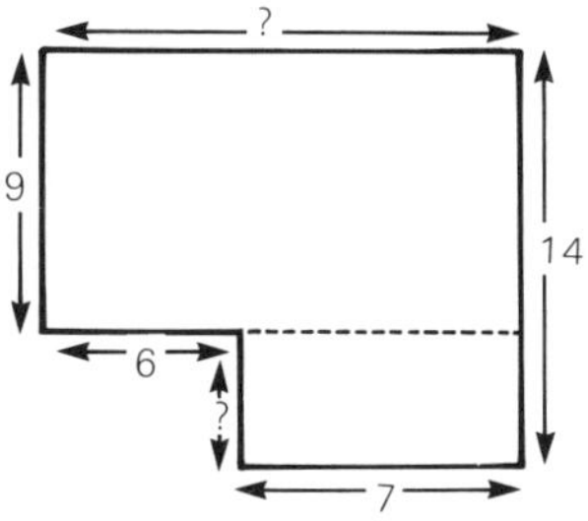

c)

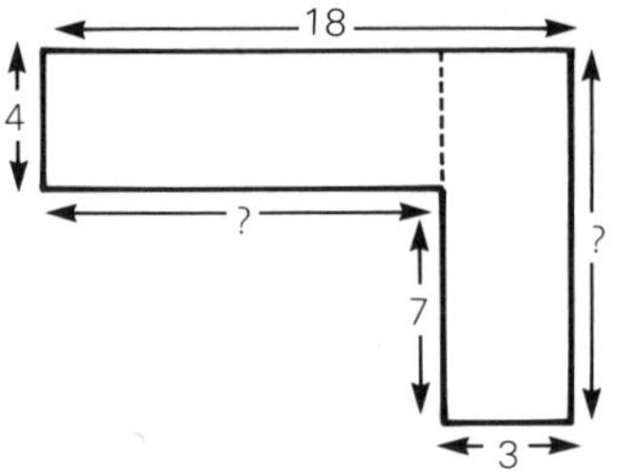

7

Find the area of each of the diagrams below (all measurements are in cm):

a)

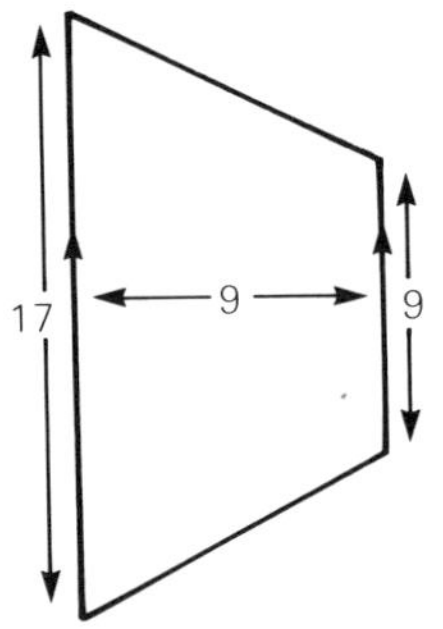

b)

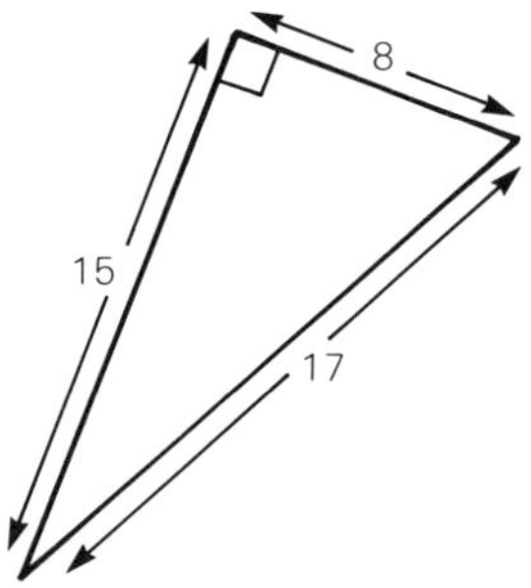

c)

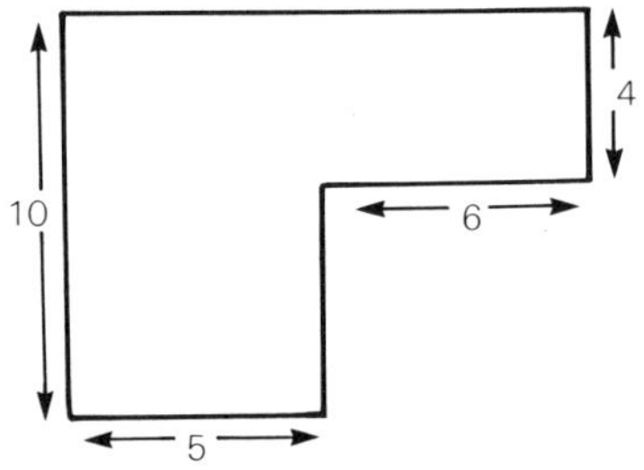

d) Find the dotted area. The border is 3 cm wide all round.

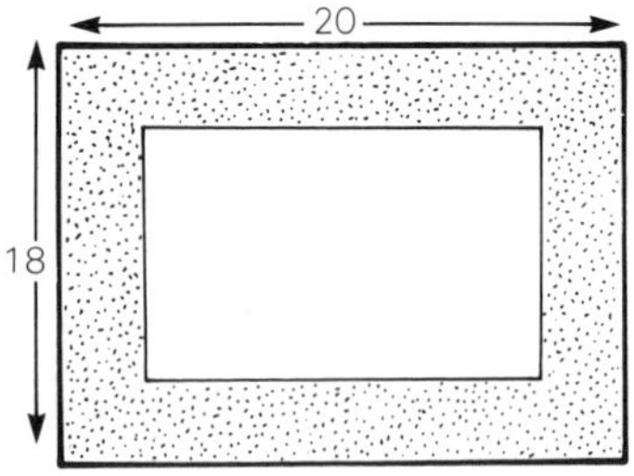

e)

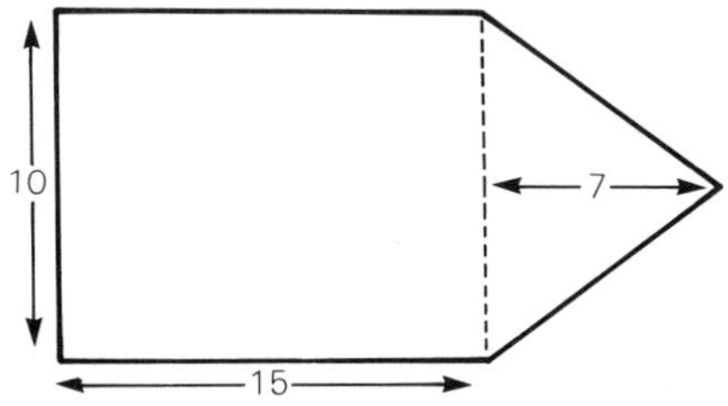

PRACTICE 2 (BCD)

1

The diagrams below show various balances. Write down the masses that the arrows are pointing to.

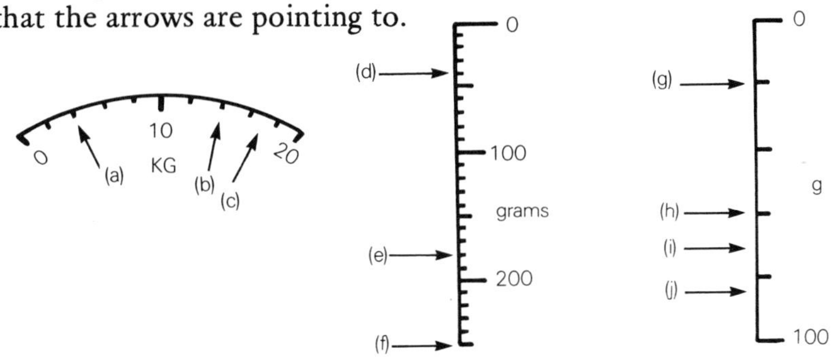

2

Using grams, guess sensibly the mass of:

a) a slice of bread

b) a cricket or hockey ball

c) an orange

d) a 50 p piece

3

The diagram below shows the county of Norfolk. The side of each square represents 10 km.

a) What is the area in km^2 of a square which is 10 km by 10 km?

b) By counting squares find the area of Norfolk in km^2.

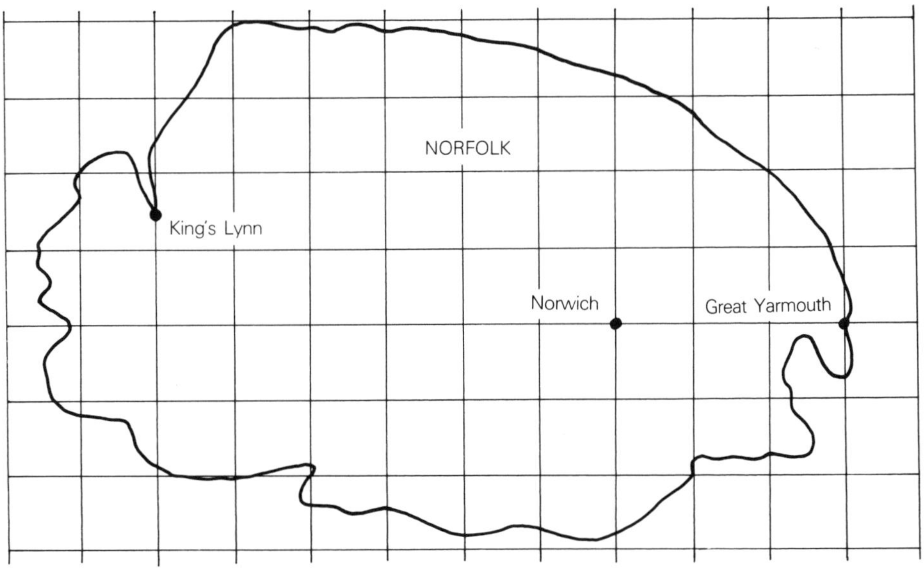

4

a) A matchbox is 5 cm long, 4 cm wide and 2 cm thick. What is its volume in cm^3?

b) A paperback book is 20 cm long, 12 cm wide and 3 cm thick. What is its volume in cm^3?

c) A paddling pool is 8 m long, 5 m wide and 0.5 m deep. What is the volume of water (in m^3) that it will hold? If it helps, think of 0.5 m as $\frac{1}{2}$ m.

d) Look at the room you are in now. Write down a sensible guess of its length, width and height in metres, using whole numbers of metres. From your guesses work out the volume of the room in m^3.

5

Look at the two bottles of shampoo opposite and work out the cost of:

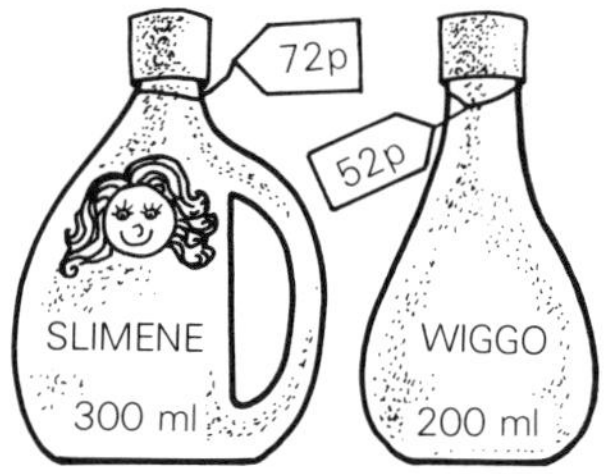

a) 100 ml of Slimene

b) 100 ml of Wiggo.

Which of the two is better value?

6

a) Find the volume of a block of iron, 2 cm by 4 cm by 5 cm.

b) 1 cm^3 of iron has a mass of 8 g. What is the mass of the block?

c) Another block of iron is 6 cm by 8 cm by 10 cm. What would its mass be?

7

Some people think that air has no weight. In fact (as you learn in science) 1 m^3 of air has a mass of about 1.3 kg.

A school hall is 20 m long, 10 m wide and 6 m high. Find its volume, and then find the mass of air it contains.

SUMMARY

1

The diagram shows a living room:

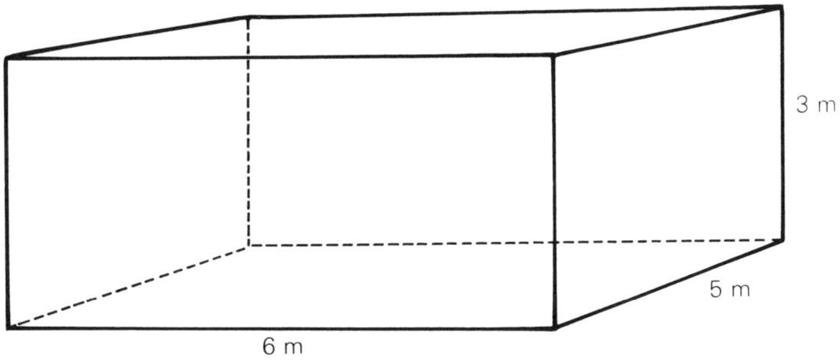

a) I want to cover the entire floor with carpet. How many m^2 of carpet will I need? If 1 m^2 of carpet costs £9, how much will the carpet cost?

b) Find the total area of the 4 walls. (Don't worry about doors and windows.) If 1 tin of emulsion paint covers 12 m^2, how many tins should I buy to paint the walls? (You can only buy whole tins.)

2

Find the area of each of the three diagrams (all measurements are in cm):

a)

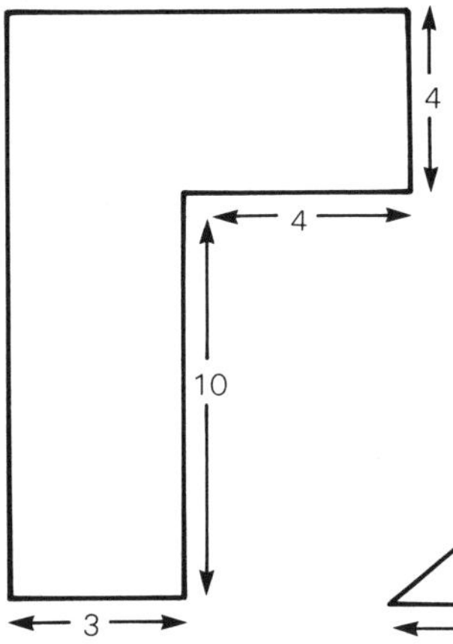

b)

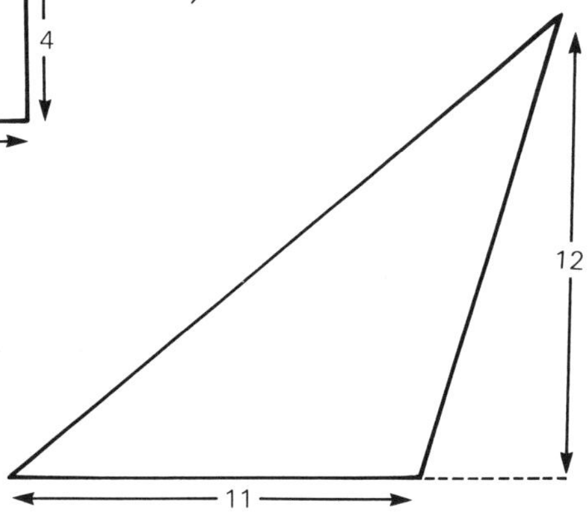

c) 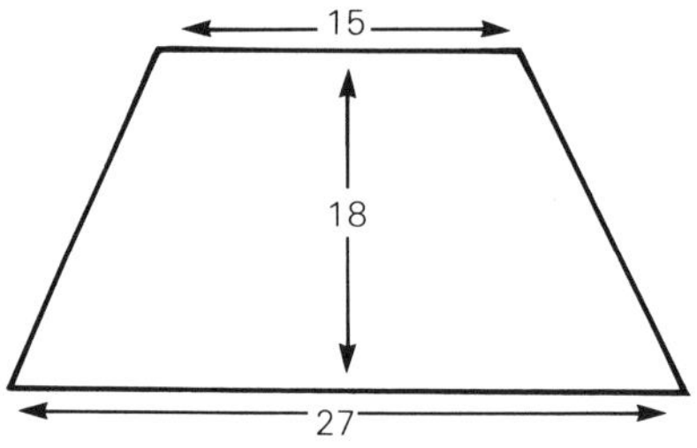

3

To get a rough idea of her volume, Morag imagines she is a cuboid 20 cm by 20 cm by 150 cm. Assuming this, what is her volume in cm^3? Remembering that $1000\ cm^3 = 1$ litre, what is her volume in litres?

4

a) A lawn is 7 m long and 5 m wide. All around it is a path 1 m wide. What is the area of the path? (It will help to make a sketch.)

b) (A hard question – don't spend too long on it.) Another lawn is 12 m long and 8 m wide. It also has a path all around it, and it just so happens that the area of the path is exactly the same as the area of the lawn. How wide is the path?

5

Find the volumes of cuboids:

a) 2 cm by 4 cm by 10 cm
b) 0.6 m by 0.7 m by 1 m
c) 20 cm by 30 cm by 40 cm
d) 2.5 cm by 3 cm by 6 cm
e) 1.5 m by 0.8 m by 3 m
f) 80 cm by 2 m by 3 m (answer in m^3).

6

Imagine that the diagram below has been cut from a piece of card.

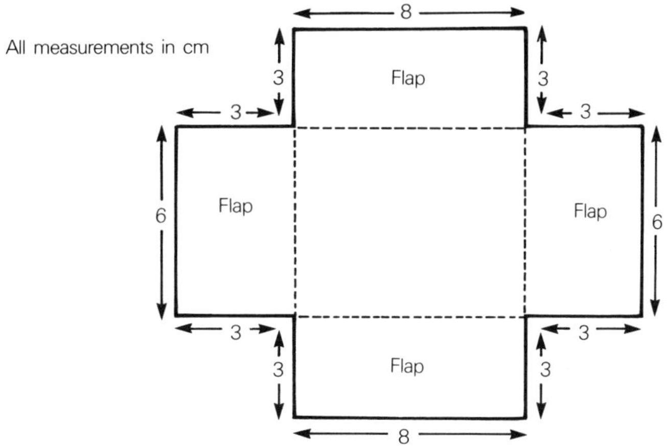

a) Find its perimeter in metres.

b) Find its area in cm^2.

c) If the 4 flaps were folded up, a box without a top would be made. What would be the volume of this box?

ALLSORTS

1

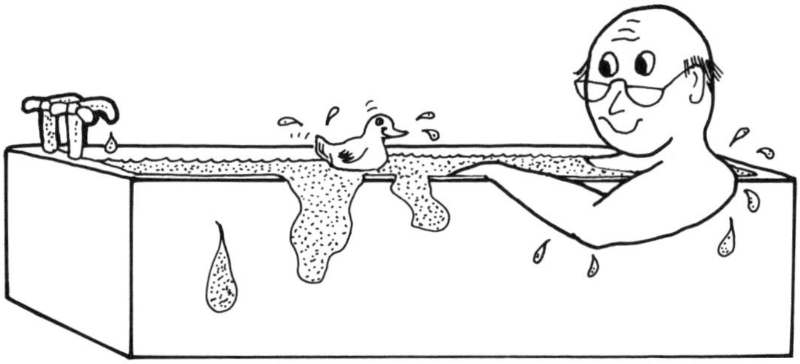

Everything in Professor Mildew's house has to have a proper mathematical shape, regardless of comfort. For example, his bath is a perfect cuboid – its base is 150 cm by 80 cm.

Before the Professor got in the bath, the water came 40 cm up the bath. After he got in, and got completely under the water, it came 50 cm up the bath.

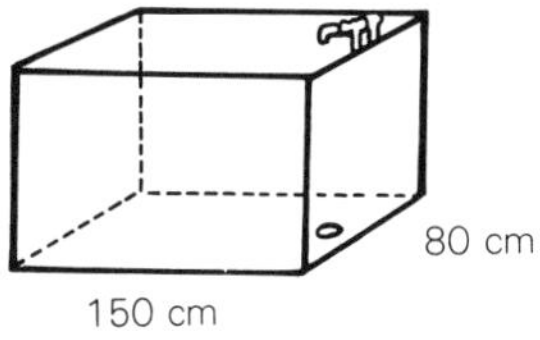

Find the Professor's volume:

a) in cm^3 b) in litres

2

a) How many dominoes 4 cm by 2 cm could you fit into a box which is 16 cm by 8 cm? You can only put 1 layer in the box. Draw a rectangle 16 squares by 8 squares and actually draw the dominoes inside it.

b) How many dominoes 5 cm by 3 cm could you fit into a box which is 16 cm by 8 cm? You can't cut dominoes up, so you have to fit them in wasting as little space as possible. Draw a diagram to show this.

3

Emma cut some shapes from the same piece of cardboard. The one on the left had a mass of 10 g. What should the mass of the one on the right be?

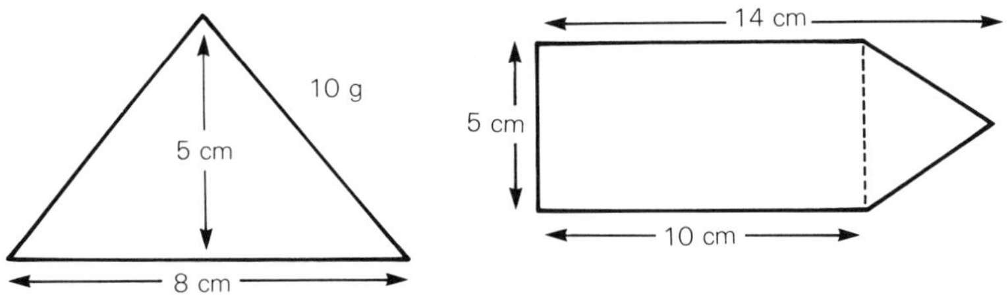

4

You have a pair of scales and four "weights": 1 g, 3 g, 9 g and 27 g.

You could weigh an object of mass 19 g like this:

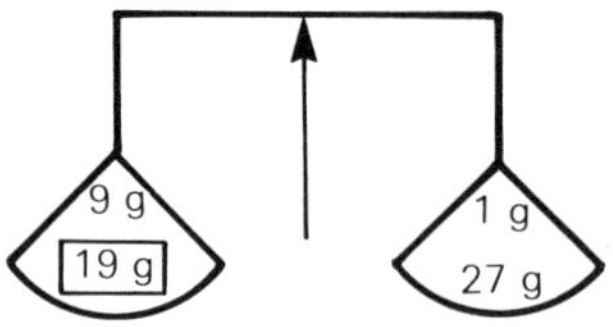

Draw similar diagrams to show how you could weigh objects of mass:

a) 11 g b) 32 g c) 16 g.

5

A curious plant (whose Latin name is "Fictio Mathematica") has leaves which are exact rectangles. What is more, a well-watered specimen has leaves which grow 1 cm in each direction every day. So a leaf might grow like this:

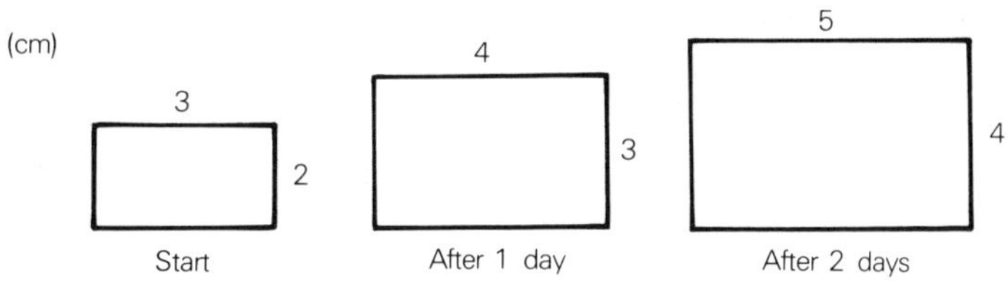

and so on.

a) What would be the area of the leaf shown 7 days after the start?

b) After how many days from the start would the leaf first have an area of over 200 cm^3?

c) Another leaf I saw had an area of 36 cm^2. What is the *least* amount that the area could be 4 days later? (**Hint**: there are several different rectangles whose areas are 36 cm^2; work them out, and think which will show the least growth of area.)

6

a) A little cube of gold, 1 cm in each direction, has a mass of 19 g. What would be the mass of a little cube of gold 2 cm in each direction? (The answer is not 38 g.)

b) Another cube of gold has a mass of 4104 g. How long is each of its sides? (**Hint**: $4104 = 19 \times 216$.)

c) 1 g of gold is worth £7. What would be the value of a cube of gold 1 m (that is 100 cm) in each direction?

7

The shape on the right has a perimeter of 10 cm and an area of 4 cm^2.

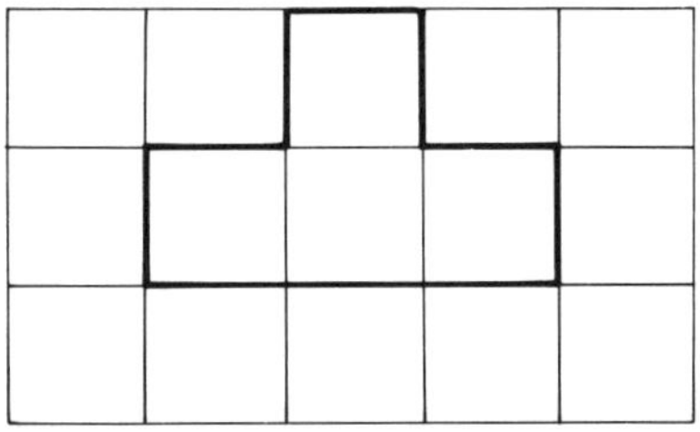

Draw shapes which have:

a) perimeter 12 cm, area 5 cm^2

b) perimeter 12 cm, area 9 cm^2

c) perimeter 14 cm, area 6 cm^2

d) perimeter 16 cm, area 7 cm^2.

14. SUBSTITUTION

PRACTICE 1 (AB)

1

If $a = 2$, $b = 5$ and $c = 3$, find the values of these expressions:

a) $3a - b + c$ **b)** $a + b - \frac{c}{2}$ **c)** $\frac{b + c}{b - c}$ **d)** $5c - 3b$

2

Tom has invented a brilliant new system of substitution: a capital letter (like G) is always worth double a small letter (like g). So for instance if $r = 3$ then $R = 6$.

> WARNING: NO ONE ELSE IN THE WORLD FOLLOWS TOM'S BRILLIANT SYSTEM!

If $t = 2$ and $U = 8$, work out Tom's values for:

a) $2T - t$ **b)** $u - T$ **c)** $\frac{T + U}{2}$ **d)** $3t - u + 2U$

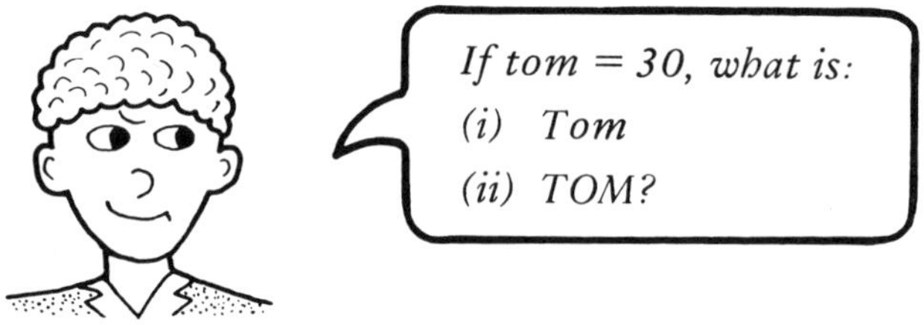

3

Answer these short questions:

a) If $m = 7$ and $n = 1$ what is the value of $2m - 5n$?

b) If $f = 3$, $g = 4$ and $h = 0$, what is the value of $3f - g + 7h$?

c) If $y = 3$ what is the value of $\frac{20}{y+1}$?

d) If $a + b$ has the value 7, and $a + 2b$ has the value 9, what are the values of a and b?

e) If $p = 7$ and $q = 9$ what is the value of $100 - 3p - 2q$?

4

Copy out the following questions, putting the correct numbers in place of the question marks. There are some examples in the box on the right to help you.

$r = 3$ and $s = 2$.	
Question	$2r + 5s = ?$
Answer	$2r + 5s = 16$
Question	$?r + 2s = 19$
Answer	$5r + 2s = 19$

In each part of the question $m = 6$ and $n = 7$.

a) $m + 2n = ?$

b) $3m - 2n + 1 = ?$

c) $?n - m = 15$

d) $6m - ?n = 1$

e) $3m + n - ? = 10$

f) $\frac{2m + 4n}{?} = 8$

g) Fill in two whole numbers so that:

$$?m + ?n = 50$$

5

Look at the "substitution square" below.

	$a = 2$, $b = 5$, $c = 1$	$a = 3$, $b = 4$, $c = 2$	$a = 1$, $b = 0$, $c = 0$	$a = 6$, $b = 10$, $c = 8$
$4a - b + c$				
$\frac{a + b + c}{2}$		$4\frac{1}{2}$		
$a + b - 2c$				
$a + \frac{b}{2} - \frac{c}{2}$				7

$4\frac{1}{2}$ has been written in that particular square because if $a = 3$, $b = 4$ and $c = 2$ then the value of $\frac{a+b+c}{2} = 4\frac{1}{2}$.

Make sure you understand why 7 has been put in the other square, then copy out the whole square and fill in the other 14 places.

PRACTICE 2 (CD)

1

"Think of a number, add 5, multiply by 3, subtract 6, divide by 3."

a) Copy the flow chart below, filling in the gaps shown by question marks.

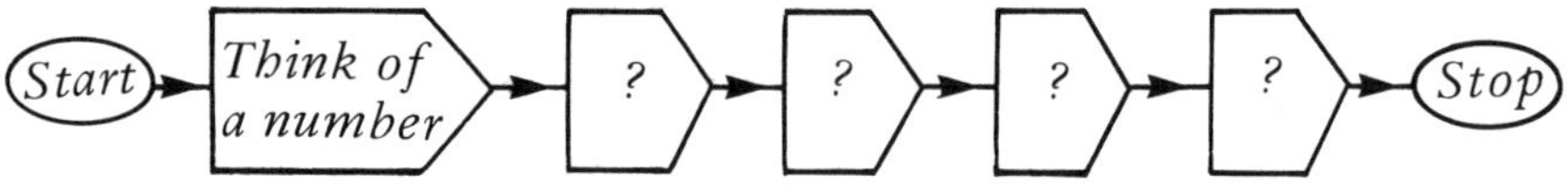

b) Put the following numbers through the flow chart, filling in all the stages. (The first has been done for you.)

6 → *11* → *33* → *27* → *9*
4
9
20

c) If the final result was 16, what was the starting number?

2

Make a flow chart for each of these:

a) "Think of a number, add twelve, multiply by 4, take away 6, divide by 2."

b) "Think of a number, double it, add 10, divide by 2."

3

If $g = 4$ and $k = 5$, find the values of:

a) $g + k - 3$ b) $5g - 3k$ c) $\frac{8g - k}{3}$

4

If we have to: "Think of a number, add 4, multiply by 5," we can make a flow chart, and underneath it we can follow through the stages for any number, x:

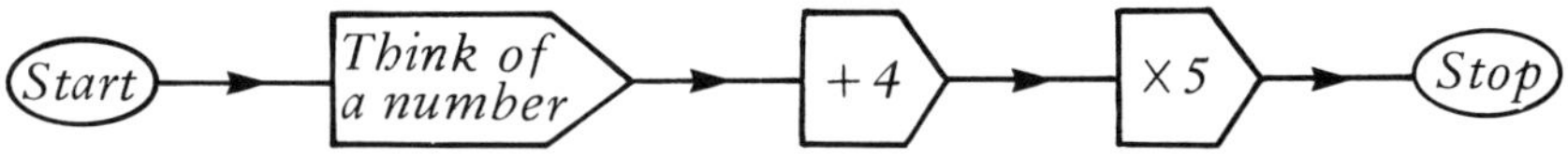

x $\quad (x+4) \quad 5(x+4)$

Do exactly the same for these:

a) "Think of a number, multiply by 2, take away 7."

b) "Think of a number, add 6, divide by 2."

c) "Think of a number, divide by 2, add 6."

5

Hamish has invented the ultimate number puzzle. The instructions for it are given in the box.

What is the final result if these are the starting numbers:

a) 11 b) 8 c) 14

d) 20?

Think of a number
↓
Multiply by 4
↓
Subtract 2
↓
Divide by 2
↓
Add 5
↓
Multiply by 3
↓
Add 6
↓
Divide by 6

SUMMARY

1

If $c=5$, $d=8$, $e=2$, $f=1$ and $g=0$, find the values of:

a) $2d-e+4g$ b) $\frac{1}{2}d+f-c$ c) $127f-619g$

d) $\frac{20}{c}+1$ e) $\frac{c+f}{e}$ f) $\frac{c+d+e+f}{4}$

2

Referring to Hamish's number puzzles, we can think of them in three ways:

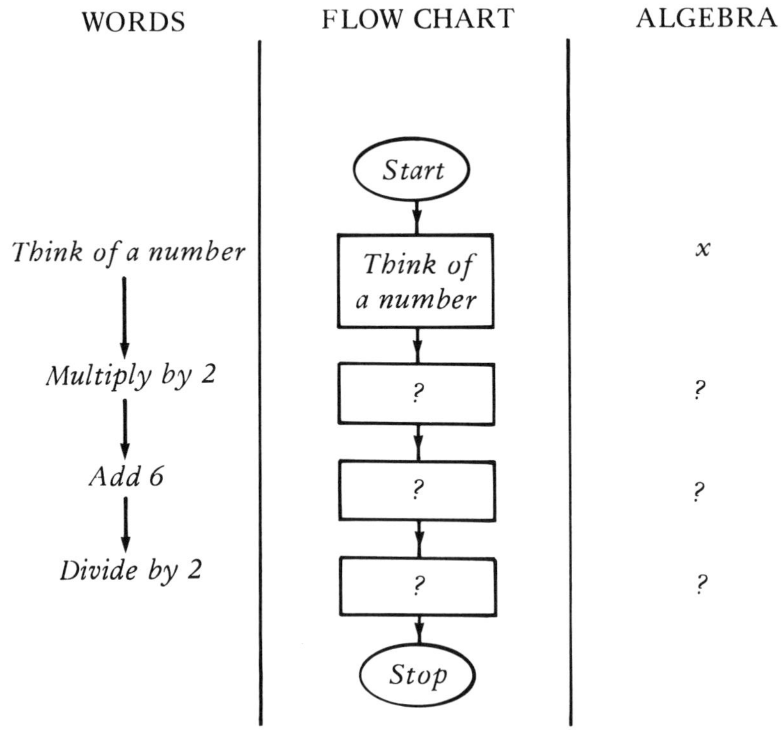

a) Copy the three columns above, putting the correct things in place of the question marks.

b) Put 6, 3 and 10 through the "WORDS" column

c) What is the connection between the final result and the number you started with?

d) Look at the last thing you have written in the "ALGEBRA" column. Why does it help you to explain your answer to (c)?

3

You already know that $2q$ means "2 times q", so it will come as no surprise to find that pq means "p times q".

Remembering this, if $p = 3$, $q = 5$, $r = 0$ and $s = 2$, find the values of:

a) pq b) qp c) ps d) qr

e) $ps + q$ f) $p - rs$ g) $\frac{ps}{2}$ h) pqs

4

If $q=5$, $r=3$, $s=2$, $t=0$, $u=\frac{1}{2}$, find the values of:

a) r^2s **b)** qs^2u **c)** $q^3t+r^4s^2$ **d)** $5s^2q \div q^2$

e) s^q **f)** $s^2u^2+q^2-rs^5u^2$

5

While doing one of Hamish's number puzzles, Emma thought of 2 and Tom thought of 3.

Here are the numbers they got as they did it:

Emma	*2*	*8*	*16*	*8*	*6*	*3*
Tom	*3*	*12*	*20*	*10*	*8*	*4*

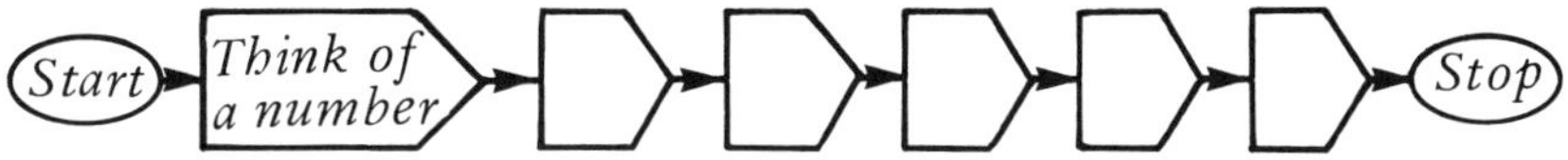

Copy and complete the above flow chart.

ALLSORTS

1

On the left are Tom's answers to some substitution questions. On the right are Shelley's answers to the next group of questions.

Tom

(i) $a+b=8$

(ii) $a-b=6$

(iii) $3b+c=6$

(iv) $\frac{c+d}{2}=4$

(v) $3a-4d=1$

Shelley

(vi) $2b+3c=$ ~~8~~ ~~11~~ 7

(vii) $\frac{b+d}{3}=2$

(viii) $cd=8$

(ix) $2a-3b+5d=$ ~~10~~ 3 ~~4~~ 6

(x) $\frac{a+3c}{2}=$ ~~16~~ 8

a) Tom's answers were all correct. Work out the values that a, b, c and d must have had.

b) Use your answers to (a) to find out which of his 5 questions Shelley got right. (Remember for example, that pq means "p times q".)

2

Hamish has been inflicting yet another of his puzzles on his friends. Boffin started with 5 and ended with 6. Fatima started with 4 and wrote down each step in case she forgot:

$$4 \longrightarrow 8 \longrightarrow 16 \longrightarrow 4$$

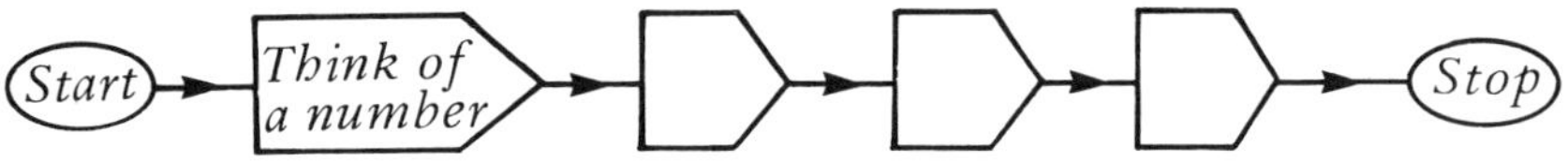

Copy and complete this flow chart for the puzzle:

Remember, the flow chart has got to fit in with Boffin's answer too.

3

Tom has carried on his original substitution idea so that every letter of the alphabet has a number value (given in the box on the right).

So, every word can be given a number:

maths = 13 + 1 + 20 + 8 + 19 = 61

He tried a couple more, which you should do too:

a) thick

b) mr abel (don't worry about capitals.)

a = 1	n = 14
b = 2	o = 15
c = 3	p = 16
d = 4	q = 17
e = 5	r = 18
f = 6	s = 19
g = 7	t = 20
h = 8	u = 21
i = 9	v = 22
j = 10	w = 23
k = 11	x = 24
l = 12	y = 25
m = 13	z = 26

He immediately made up a theory that words that have the same number must be connected. Then he tried:

c) fool d) tom

e) clever f) boring

and that quickly led him to abandon his theory.

Now try these words (and any others you like): fat, silly, daft, pretty, stupid, clown, zombie, mad, bright.

You might like to compare them with names of friends, teachers, school subjects, etc.

15. LOCUS

PRACTICE 1 (ABC)

Mr Toad's goat tends to find himself tied up in all sorts of strange fields and positions. In the diagrams below, the goat is shown by the letter G.

1

Normally he is tethered to a peg in the ground by a rope 5 m long. This peg is 4 m from a long wall.

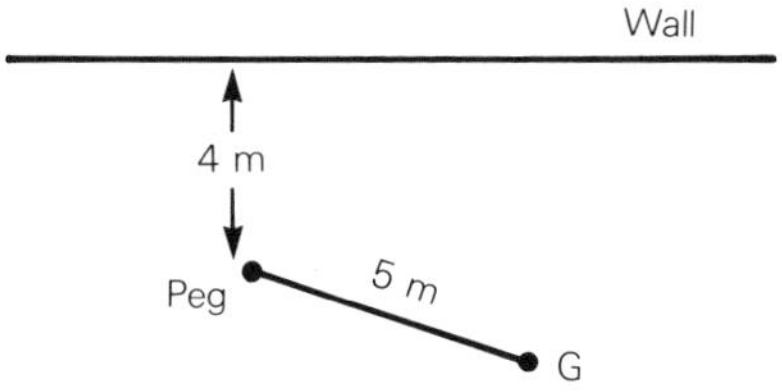

Make a scale drawing of the wall and the peg. It doesn't really matter how long you make the wall – about 10 cm will do. Use a scale of 1 cm to 1 m.

Now:

a) Using your compasses, shade the area of grass the goat can reach.

b) Write down what length of the wall (in metres) the goat can reach.

2

Sometimes the goat is tied to a nail stuck in the side of a broad tree trunk. The diagram opposite shows the position, looking down from above.

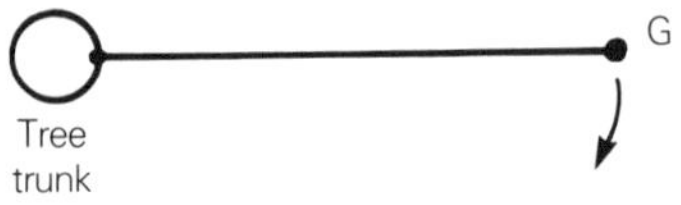

For each part of this question, make a copy of the diagram about the same size as the one above. It is not a scale drawing, just a sketch.

a) The goat starts walking in a kind of clockwise circle (in the direction of the arrow), always keeping the rope tightly stretched. Make a sketch of his path (or locus) as he gradually wraps himself round the tree.

b) Make a sketch showing the area of grass the goat can reach. (This time he can go clockwise or anticlockwise, as he likes.)

3

Another field in which the goat occasionally gets imprisoned is a perfect equilateral triangle. Each side is 8 m long. He gets tied to a peg in the middle of one of the sides.

a) Using a scale of 1 cm to 1 m make a scale drawing of the field and the peg.

b) Honeysuckle grows along the other two walls. The goat doesn't like honeysuckle – in fact he can't stand the stuff – but if he could reach it he would certainly eat it out of pure mischief. What is the longest length of rope he can safely be tied with, so that he can't quite reach the honeysuckle? Shade the area of grass he can reach if he is tied with this rope.

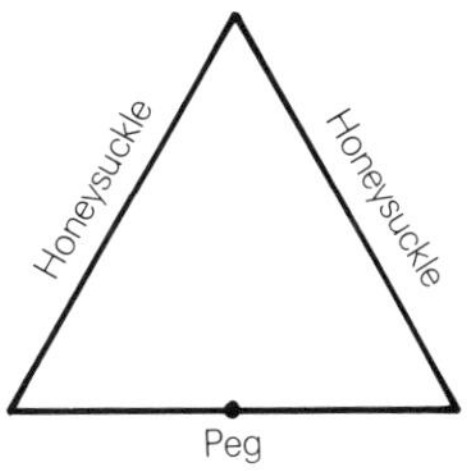

4

Yet another small field is a rectangle 8 m by 6 m. It has two pegs in it – one in a corner, the other half-way along one of the sides.

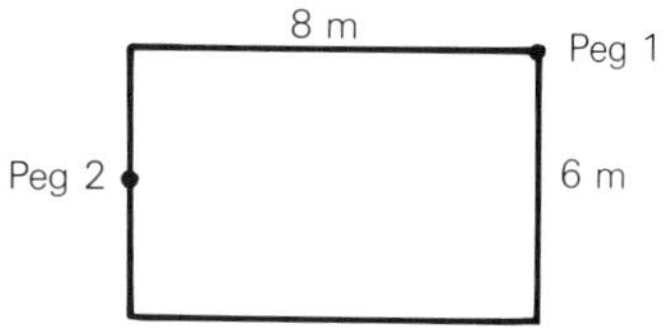

a) Using a scale of 1 cm to 1 m, make a scale drawing of the field, putting in the two pegs.

b) Sometimes the goat is tied by a 5 m rope from peg 1. Shade the area of grass he can eat like this: 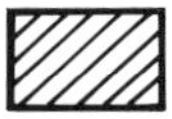

c) At other times he is tied by a 5 m rope from peg 2. Shade the area of grass he can eat like this: 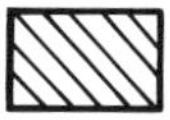

d) Sometimes the unfortunate beast is tied by a 5 m rope from peg 1 and at the same time by a 5 m rope from peg 2. Shade the area of grass he could eat then like this: 

PRACTICE 2 (DE)

1

Professor Mildew's living room is 7 m long and 5 m wide. One of the shorter walls is completely covered by a bookshelf. The fireplace is in the middle of one of the longer walls.

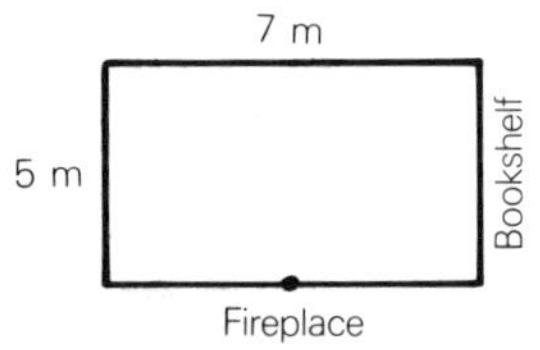

The Professor insists on having his armchair less than 2.5 m from the fire, and less than 2 m from the bookshelf.

Make a scale drawing of the living room (1 cm to 1 m), and shade the area in which the Professor could put his armchair.

2

On the next page is a scale drawing of the Maths Room at Subset House School.

The 24 crosses show the positions of the children in the class. The dot shows the position of Mr Abel, who is standing with his back to the class writing on the blackboard. A paper pellet has just hit him on the back of the head. He has a lot of experience in this sort of thing, and is certain it was fired from a desk more than 3.5 m from him, but less than 4 m from him.

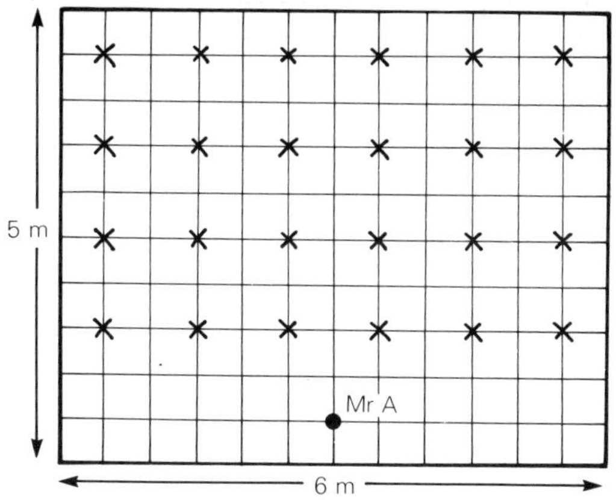

Make an exact copy of the scale drawing, and circle the desks of the possible culprits.

3

For each part of this question you must draw a new square of side 5 cm, labelling the corners like the diagram opposite. Shade only points inside the square.

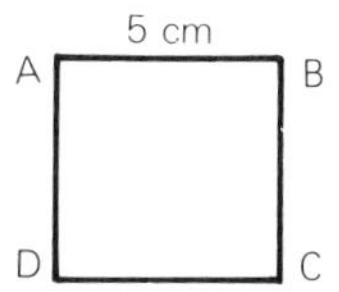

a) Shade the set of points more than 6 cm from the point B.

b) Shade the set of points less than 2 cm from the line AB.

c) Shade the set of points less than 3 cm from the point C and less than 3 cm from the point D.

d) Shade the set of points less than 1 cm from the line AC.

e) Shade the set of points less than 3 cm from the line AB and less than 3 cm from the line CD.

f) Shade the set of points more than 2 cm but less than 3 cm from the point D.

g) (A little complicated!) Shade the set of points less than 1 cm from the line BD, and more than 3 cm from the point A, and less than 4 cm from both B and D.

SUMMARY

1

The diagram on the next page shows the centre of the village of Much Snoring.

a) Using a scale of 1 cm to 100 m, make a scale drawing of the village.

b) A man wants to buy a house which is less than 500 m from the station and less than 400 m from the High Street. Shade that area on your scale drawing.

c) If he does buy a house in this area, what is the furthest distance he can be from the pub?

2

For each part of this question draw a circle of radius 4 cm, and mark the centre, O, and the points X and Y.

a) Shade the set of points inside the circle which are more than 2 cm from the line XY.

b) Shade the set of points inside the circle which are more than 5 cm from X but less than 2 cm from O.

c) Shade the set of points in the circle which are more than 3 cm from O but less than 1 cm from the line XY.

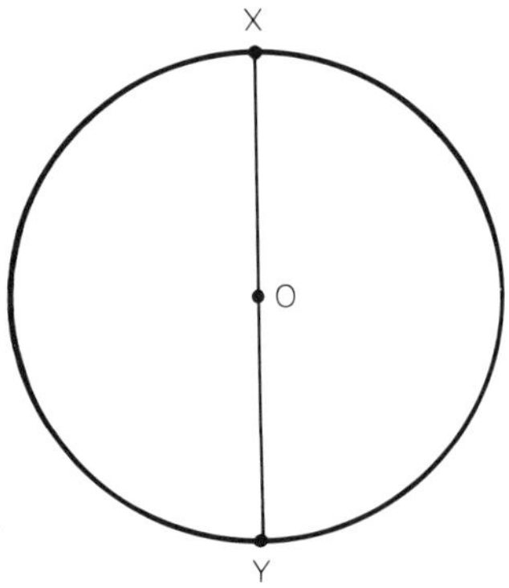

3

Mr Toad has been shopping and bought two new goats, much to the disgust of the original goat (goat 1 as he has to be called now).

All three goats are kept in the same field, which is 10 m by 8 m. Goat 1 is tied to peg 1 by a rope 4 m long; goat 2 is tied to peg 2 by a rope 7 m long; goat 3 is tied to peg 3 by a rope 8 m long.

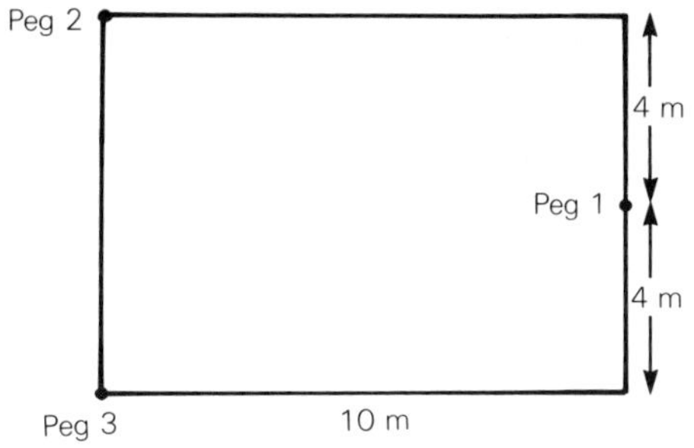

Make a scale drawing of the field (1 cm to 1 m). Use your compasses to mark out the "territory" of each goat.

a) Put a letter "a" in the region where all three goats could meet for a chat.

b) Put a letter "b" in the region where goat 2 and goat 3 could meet out of the range of goat 1.

c) Put a letter "c" in each of the regions which none of the three goats can reach.

d) Put a letter "d" in the region where goat 1 can be completely on his own (which is what he likes best).

e) By drawing and counting squares, find which goat has the greatest area of grass completely to himself.

ALLSORTS

1

Another of Mr Toad's fields is very large, but in the middle it has a rectangle of iron railing 8 m long and 6 m wide.

Goat 1 is tied to this railing by a rope which has a loop at the other end which can slide along the railing. The diagram shows some of the positions goat 1 could take up. The rope is 2 m long.

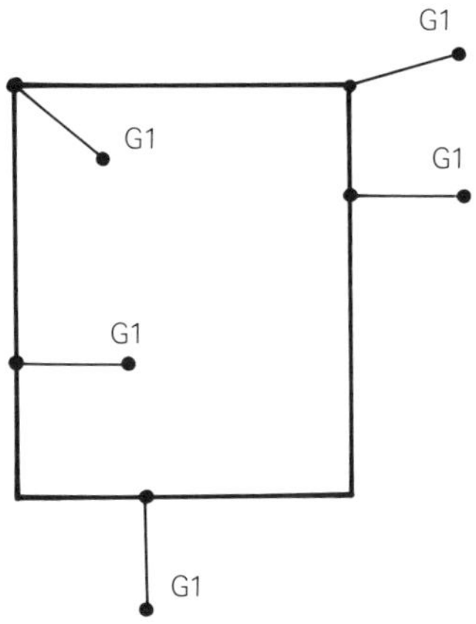

Make a scale drawing of the railing (1 cm to 1 m) and shade the area of grass goat 1 could reach.

What is the area of the patch of grass inside the railing which the goat cannot reach?

2

BC is a line 9 cm long. How could you find a point which is 3.2 cm from C and 6.4 cm from B? The arcs on the diagram give you a hint.

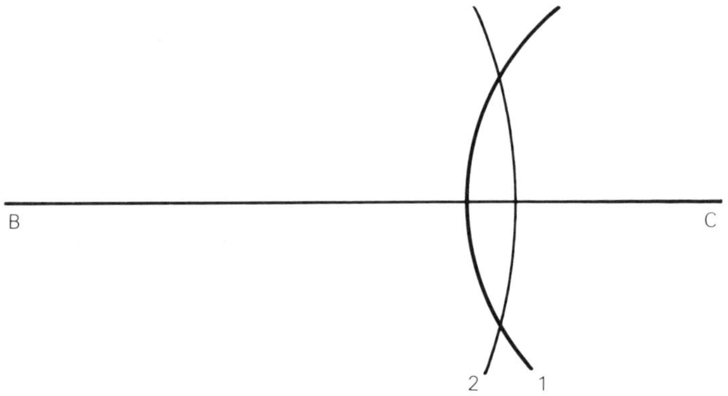

The answer is: open your compasses to 3.2 cm, put the point on C and draw an arc (number 1 on the diagram); now open your compasses to 6.4 cm, put the point on B and draw another arc; where the arcs cross are the correct points – and, as you can see, there are 2 of them.

Make sure you understand this before you go on to the problem below.

In Mr Abel's garden there is a beech tree, B, and a cherry tree, C. Mr Abel, A, is 6 m from B and 3 m from C, doing long multiplication in his head.

Suddenly he notices that he is twice as far from B as from C, and wonders what his locus would look like if he took a stroll, always staying twice as far from B as from C.

a) *In the middle of a new page*, make a scale drawing, scale 1 cm to 1 m, showing A, B and C.

b) Mark the two points (call them Q_1 and Q_2) which are 3.2 cm from C and 6.4 cm from B.

c) Now mark the two points (R_1 and R_2) which are 3.5 cm from C and 7 cm from B.

d) Now mark the two points (S_1 and S_2) which are 4 cm from C and 8 cm from B.

Carry on in the same way:

T_1 and T_2: 4.5 cm from C and 9 cm from B

U_1 and U_2: 5 cm from C and 10 cm from B

V_1 and V_2: 5.5 cm from C and 11 cm from B

W_1 and W_2: 6 cm from C and 12 cm from B

X_1 and X_2: 6.5 cm from C and 13 cm from B.

Finally join up all the points you have marked with as smooth a curve as you can manage. It should look something like this:

3

With Mr Abel, one idea tends to lead to another. He goes back to his original position:

This time he wonders what his locus would look like if, instead, he always kept 3 m further from B than from C.

Rather as you did in Question 2, mark his position when he is:

6.5 cm from B and 3.5 cm from C
7 cm from B and 4 cm from C
7.5 cm from B and 4.5 cm from C

and so on, as far as you can manage.

Again, join them up with a smooth curve.

16. FRACTIONS IV

PRACTICE 1 (A)

1

Multiply:

a) 2.1×0.6 b) 5.4×0.7 c) 0.4×0.66 d) 12.6×0.03

e) 0.4×24 f) 2.88×0.02

2

Work out the answers to the problems underneath this price list:

PRICE PER KG

Cheese	£2.50	Sugar	£0.48
Steak	£4.30	Carrots	£0.28
Mushrooms	£1.30	Plums	£0.55

a) How much will 0.6 kg of cheese cost? (The sum to do is 0.6×2.5. Don't forget to write the answer properly as money.)

b) How much will 2.5 kg of sugar cost?

c) To make plum jam, Mrs Haddock, the school cook, needs:

0.6 kg plums 0.5 kg sugar

How much will this cost altogether?

d) A large steak weighs 0.4 kg. How much will it cost?

e) Mrs Mildew sent the Professor to the shops to buy 2.5 kg of carrots. Unfortunately he bought 5.2 kg of mushrooms instead.

(i) How much would he have spent if he had bought the carrots as he was told?

(ii) How much did he spend, in fact?

3

Work out

a) 0.4×0.5 b) 0.2×0.3 c) 1.1×0.7 d) 0.05×0.9

e) 0.8×0.8 f) 0.65×0.6

4

Find the area of each of these rectangles:

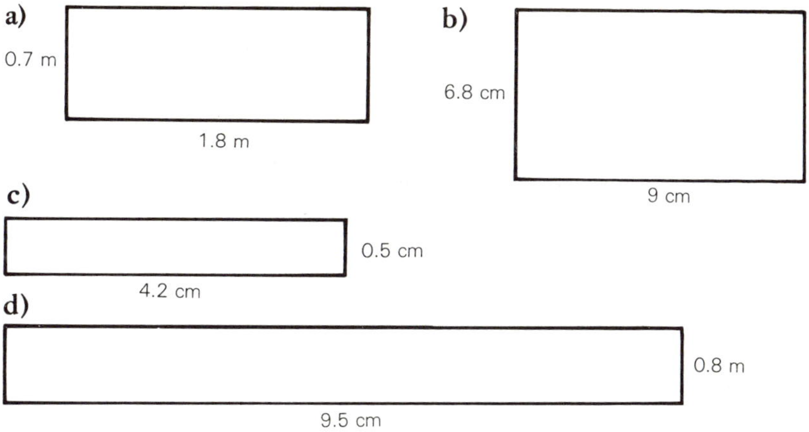

PRACTICE 2 (BC)

1

Do these divisions. The numbers are easy – it's the decimal point you must be very careful about.

a) $\frac{0.06}{0.2}$ b) $\frac{2.8}{0.4}$ c) $\frac{0.48}{0.6}$ d) $\frac{0.072}{1.2}$

e) $\frac{1.4}{0.02}$ f) $\frac{12}{0.8}$

2

Do these divisions. Remember, first write them out like the ones in Question 1.

a) $6.6 \div 0.3$ b) $12.6 \div 1.4$ c) $0.26 \div 1.3$ d) $3.06 \div 0.06$

e) $0.132 \div 2.2$ f) $0.4 \div 0.25$

3

Mr Abel knew he was going to be a few minutes late for class, so he left a question on the board for the children to do. Unfortunately someone (everyone suspects it was Egbert) rubbed out the sign between the two numbers.

a) Shelley, the laziest boy in the school, did this sum:

$$6 + 0.25$$

b) Fatima was sure it should have been:

$$6 - 0.25$$

c) Hamish was anxious to use his amazing discovery about multiplying decimals, so he did:

$$6 \times 0.25$$

d) Emma was rather proud of the fact that she could do division of decimals without using a calculator, so she did:

$$6 \div 0.25$$

What answer should each of them have got?

4

a) A 5 p piece is 0.17 cm thick. Boffin has a pile of 5 p pieces which is 2.9 cm high. How many 5 p pieces do you think there are in the pile?

b) It takes 2.4 m of cloth to make a shirt. How many shirts could be made from a roll of cloth 60 m long?

c) Cheese costs £2.50 per kilogram. A large piece of cheese cost £4.50. How many kilograms did it weigh?

5

Do these division questions:

a) $2.68 \div 0.4$ b) $0.255 \div 1.5$ c) $1.7 \div 0.04$

d) $0.075 \div 0.6$ e) $18 \div 1.2$ f) $0.063 \div 0.18$

SUMMARY

1

Boffin's latest project is to paint one whole wall of his bedroom with silver paint. (His mother doesn't know about it yet!) The diagram shows the size of the wall. You can only get small tins of silver paint, and it says on the side of the tin that, "one tin is sufficient to cover $2.5\ m^2$." A tin cost £1.85.

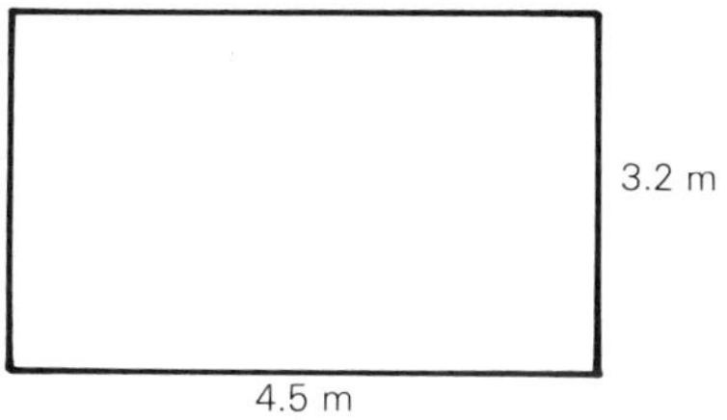

a) What is the area of Boffin's wall?

b) Work out exactly, as a decimal, how many tins Boffin would need.

c) Of course, you can only buy a whole number of tins. How many should Boffin buy, and what would be the total cost?

2

Do these 10 short decimal questions. *Pay special attention to the decimal point.*

a) 2.4×1.6 b) $8 - 3.75$ c) $6 + 2.6 + 0.73$

d) $4 \div 1.6$ e) $0.2 \times 1.2 \times 1.5$ f) $(7 \times 0.63) - 2$

g) $0.12 \div 1.5$ h) $(2-0.15)\times 1.6$ i) $\dfrac{9}{0.9}-9.9$

j) $8+(8.5\times 0.6)$

3

Here is a scale drawing of a tennis court:

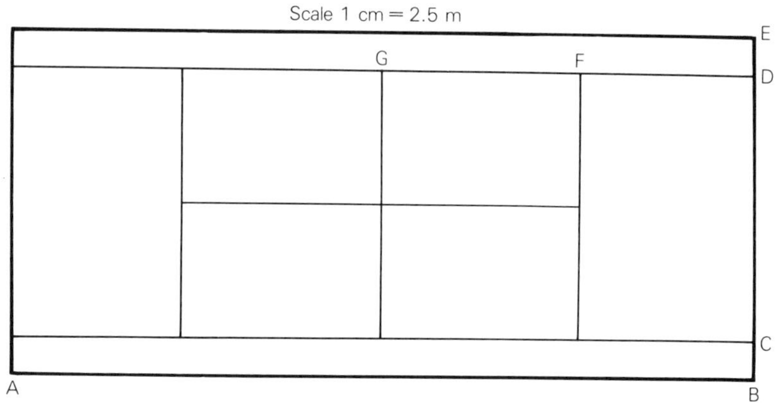

Find the lengths of these lines *in metres*. The way to do it is: measure the length in cm then multiply by 2.5 to turn the measurement into metres.

a) AB b) BE c) BC d) CD

e) DF f) FG g) AE

ALLSORTS

1

Put in signs and brackets to make these sums work. There is an example in the box to help you to see what to do.

6 0.5 0.2 = 6.1
Answer: $6+(0.5\times 0.2)=6.1$

a) 6 0.5 0.2 = 1.3 b) 6 0.5 0.2 = 3.2

c) 6 0.5 0.2 = 8.5 d) 6 0.5 0.2 = 0.6

e) 6 0.5 0.2 = 5.3

2

A twiddly pair of numbers is a pair of numbers that multiply together to make a whole number.

For instance: 0.75 and 8 are a twiddly pair (because $8 \times 0.75 = 6$).
0.35 and 6 aren't twiddly (because $0.35 \times 6 = 2.1$).

Arrange these 10 numbers into twiddly pairs:

0.4 8 2.5 20 6 5 1.2 0.25 0.1 1.5

There shouldn't be any un-twiddly numbers left at the end!

3

a) Work out: $\dfrac{0.2 \times 0.3}{0.004}$

b) Work out: $0.000\,65 \times 0.006$

c) Work out: 1250×0.0008

d) Find $\sqrt{0.49}$ (that is, find the number which makes 0.49 when it is multiplied by itself).

e) Find $\sqrt{0.000\,004}$

f) Work out 0.3^3 (which means $0.3 \times 0.3 \times 0.3$).

4

Hamish has been studying very small decimal numbers — numbers like 0.005 and 0.000 007. He soon got tired of writing out noughts all the time, so he decided to write:

0.005 as 5D3 — because 5 is the 3rd number after the Decimal point

and 0.000 007 as 7D6 — because 7 is the 6th number after the Decimal point.

Write these numbers in Hamish's way:

a) 0.0002 b) 0.08 c) 0.000 000 2

Write these Hamish-numbers in the normal way:

d) 6D4 e) 4D8 f) 5D1

Work out the answers to these questions:

g) 2D5 × 3D2 h) 3D7 × 3D4

Of course, the answers should be written in Hamish's way too.